Cops, Villains and Trials

Explorations in Crime and Law for Family and Social Historians

Stephen Wade

Emerald Guides
www.straightforwardco.co.uk

© Stephen Wade 2020

All rights reserved. No part of this publication may be reproduced in a retrieval system or transmitted by any means, electronic or mechanical, photocopying or otherwise, without the prior permission of the copyright holder.

Stephen Wade has asserted the moral right to be identified as the author of this work.

British cataloguing in Publication Data. A catalogue record is available for this book from the British library.

978-1-913342-23-4

Printed by 4edge Ltd www.4edge.co.uk
Cover design by BW Studio Derby

Whilst every effort has been taken to ensure that the information in this book is accurate at the time of going to press, the author and publisher recognise that the information can become out of date. The book is therefore sold on the understanding that no responsibility for errors and omissions is assumed and no responsibility is held for the information held within.

Cops, Villains and Trials
Explorations in Crime and Law
for Family and Social Historians

Contents

	pp
Introduction	
1. Chronicles of Crime	8
2. Cops	52
3. Villains	70
4. Trials	96
5. Other Criminal Sources	125
6. Irish Themes	178
General Bibliography	207

**

Introduction

For some years now I have been working in the huge and complex area of the history of crime. This is one of the rooms in the vast mansion of historical studies that has some space for amateur enthusiasts: that is to say, writers who have no degree in law nor any experience as a police officer or other legal person. My interests in the purely social side of this subject gradually expanded into the fascinating study of family history, and these collected essays are almost all taken from my contributions to the main family history magazines. Some are from *The Family and Local History Handbook*. But I have added new material.

The focus is on offering case studies in essay form, rather than any systematic presentation of material. My intention here is to add some fascinating stories to the basic framework we all, as historical researchers, have to work with.

As the whole area of interest covered by crime and law within social history generally comprises not only the central themes of crime-investigation –trial, but an almost infinite number of ancillary topics, I always felt the need to explore some of the ramifications of legal history in this respect, and hence I have included here such topics as police court missionaries and the court for crown cases reserved: subjects of great usefulness to family historians but little known.

Overall, I hope this collection provides openings to researchers and writers looking into those 'skeletons in the cupboard' we all have somewhere, the reason being that 'crimes' in times past were

Introduction

so easy to commit that many who were in the dock c. 1750 would now be doing the same action but committing no transgression.

There is a need to explain the problems and pitfalls awaiting the family historian at this point, with particular reference to the history of crime and law. Looking into the narrative of a specific crime offers something very special to the historian; this is perhaps best explained as a light shining into a dark corner. The footnotes of history are often the areas with the most insight into the motivations of the past. The challenge we have is immense, as it is a search for the truth – or as near to the truth as we might expect to arrive at. My view is that there is always an unanswered question, and that every enquiry leads to a dozen others. A small triumph may be an immense discovery.

When my niece delved into our own family history, as a crime historian, I of course secretly desired a terrible villain to be revealed from our past. There was no such luck. The only offender found was an uncle who committed suicide, and that was only shortly before the 1961 legislation which ended suicide per se as a criminal offence (though pacts were still unlawful).

In family history, the problems and pitfalls are many, but the most common are:

Lost or destroyed records
Events with no documentation
Misread information
Journalistic errors in press reports

Specifically in crime investigation from the long annals of the law, we meet with frustrations all the time. I was once asked to try to trace a villain who had emigrated from Britain to South Africa, just after the Anglo-Boer War, and of course he had changed his name. There was very slim chance of tracking him down. But what perhaps exemplifies the nature of these frustrations and wrong turns is an example from when I first began to research history. I was looking into the famous Lincoln case of Tom Otter, and his horrendous murder of his new wife. In a contemporary newspaper report, a writer had written the Latin phrase 'nisi primis' and of course I took out the reference works and searched for this. I wasted some time before realising that what the words should have been were 'nisi prius' – meaning 'unless before' and that refers to a particular timing of a trial.

That was a caveat regarding the internet and newspaper sources. More problematic is oral history. I have always found that families have myths, distortions and delusions. Every little story-source from the past is open to interference over the process of time and change. I grew up with tales of a roving Scotsman called Argyle who arrived in South Leeds circa 1890 and married into our matrilineal line; for years I thought this was the case. Then the discovery was made that the Argyles in our story came north from Buskington in Warwickshire. They were farm labourers.

But at the heart of this aspect of family and social history is the intensely human element. In my notebooks, which have been filled during my mainstream research, with off-shoots of interest, I have this, quoted from the Annual register for 1803:

'The sessions ended at the Old Bailey when 7 malefactors received sentence of death.

Introduction

Viz. Thomas Beck and Peter Robinson for the highway; Dorothy Soffet for stealing a guinea from

A person in drink; Richard Wentland for a street robbery; Anne Wentland his wife for forcibly

... stealing goods out of a house at Hendon. Hurst was held up at the bar to receive

Sentence and died on the back of one who was carrying him to the cells. The 2 women

Pleaded their bellies; Wentland only was found pregnant; 25 ordered for transportation, 3 burnt

In the hand, and 4 to be whipped.'

Now, this reflects both the attraction and the challenge of entering that past country where they did things so very differently. The reader has to know the reasons for pleading the belly, and why people were burnt in the hand or transported. Yet under all the contextual material, there is that strong, heart-rending human presence.

**

1

Chronicles of Crime

I begin with a broad survey of crime through our history.

Summary

The years 1100 - 1500 saw massive changes in English law. The process of dealing with criminals moved from a reliance on local courts run by the manorial lords to the assize circuits – courts controlled by travelling justices working on behalf of the 'King's Peace' in his realm. Before the Norman Conquest in 1066 when William of Normandy ('The Conqueror') began the long line of Plantagenet sovereigns, the Saxon communities had worked by 'hundred courts' and *'Frankpledge.'* This meant that a small local group, led by a responsible elder or elders, would take responsibility for hearing accusations and applying punishment. By 1500 there had been a gradual evolution of statute law, with clear notions of trial and punishment. The jury had been created and justices of the peace ran the local and regional hearings.

THE ANGLO-SAXONS

All this was an amazing achievement. For the Germanic Anglo-Saxons, an assortment of laws had been listed and defined by the kings of various areas or shires. These relied on trial by ordeal or combat. Punishment was seen as a sliding scale depending on the nature of the transgression. King Ethelbert of Kent had decreed, for instance, that a murderer would have to pay a hundred shillings, but if the victim only had a facial bone smashed, then the fine would be twenty shillings.

The church was a powerful influence on criminal law and penalties were given for such offences as fornication, eating meat in a fast or doing a deal with the Devil. There was a strong tradition of both the church and the state taking fines rather than punishment, as the kings were always in need of more cash in their coffers. After Augustine landed at Thanet in 597 the church developed its own grand ideas of compensation: if goods were stolen from a holy place, then the Bishop was entitled to twelve times the value.

Particular injuries to people also involved compensation from the assailant with a similar rationale. An eye was valued at fifty shillings, a toe at six pence, and if a thumb was damaged so it had to be cut off then twenty shillings had to be paid.

KEY TERMS

Assizes The courts formalised in the reign of Edward I, later becoming the twice-yearly courts heard by the king's justices in 'circuits' of the land.

Felony An offence that resulted in the offender sacrificing all goods and lands. In this period, it meant a death sentence, and the crown would take the possessions. This forfeiture was abolished in 1870.

Frankpledge A system of preserving the peace in the early Norman period. Men were formed in groups of ten, all charged with the task of keeping 'order and number' in those ranks.

Indictment An official statement of a charge relating to a criminal offence. This Would be a document, presented to the grand jury.

THE NORMAN PERIOD

There was nothing universal here: different rulers had their own ideas of punishments.

The worst destiny for a villain in many ways was outlawry. An outlaw was a man who had been placed outside the protection of the law. A man over fourteen could be outlawed, and criminal *indictments* for treason, rebellion, conspiracy and other serious *felonies* could lead to a criminal outlawry. In civil courts, a man could be outlawed for severe debt problems.

Because both the church and the state had notions of legislation, the concept of sin was gradually absorbed into the common law. Serious crimes such as murder, rape and robbery were *torts* (wrongs) but then later were definitely sins, so there had to be penance, as in the murder of Thomas a Beckett and Henry II's long-lasting penance as he took responsibility. But generally there was an increase in severity and brutality in punishments until the first proper criminal law measures of Edward I in the thirteenth century.

COMMUNAL and MANORIAL RESONSIBILITY

We all know the word 'posse' from the western movies in which a group of men were gathered by the sheriff to help him chase and catch the robbers. In Medieval England there was a sheriff (from the word 'shire-reeve') and he was responsible for all kinds of regional legal work. One of his jobs was to assemble a *posse comitatus* to pursue the rogues on his patch. This was a group of people from the community who saw that pursuit and retribution was their task. There was also the hue and cry – the general alarm and call for help if a crime was committed.

As night-time was the most dangerous time, when families and citizens were most vulnerable, there was the concept of 'watch and ward'- the gates of walled towns being shut, and the 'Watch' was responsible for that work.

Manorial courts record all kinds of offences from the Medieval period. They are in Latin, but many have been translated by local record societies. These are usually in the form of manorial rolls, and those published have an index of names.

The 'ENGLISH JUSTINIAN'

Edward I (1272-1307) earned this nick-name, after Justinian who codified law in the later Roman Empire. Edward created the Statute of Westminster in 1275, a legal code intended to reduce the abuse of the legal system by the people within it. He also enlarged the powers of the sheriffs and 'keepers of the peace' who were to become the first 'justices of the peace in an act of 1361. In the Anglo-Saxon period there had been a *tithingman* – a person responsible for this 'hundred' of people, and the justice of the peace inherited that role, but on a larger scale.

ANARCHY AND VENDETTA

In a Yorkshire parish in 1310, Sir John Eland murdered members of the rival Beaumont family so he could have their land.

A reading of the court rolls and assize records for the fourteenth and fifteenth centuries gives a clear impression of the attitudes at the time towards crimes of violence. Murder, rape and serious assault were rife. In 1451, a gang of four hundred armed men went into the quarter sessions at Walsingham in Norfolk and took out their friends who stood accused. In 1348 in Yorkshire there were 88 cases of murder on record. One writer has calculated that today, that proportion of killings in the population would mean that there would be around ten thousand murders a year. The assize rolls contain hundreds of cases in which a man has abducted a neighbour's wife or entered a homer and raped the women, and simply had to pay a fine.

WHERE TO FIND RECORDS
Assize courts-Early assize records are at the National Archives, found at JUST 1 to JUST 4

Manorial Courts-County record offices will have manorial records: up to 1733 these were written in Latin. But historical societies of various kinds are constantly printing editions with translations and summaries of contents. The index will provide family names, and these are done by county.

Outlawry-The National Archives has the writs – calling for the appearance of the accused –found at JUST 2. Outlawries from civil proceedings are at CP 40. There are also eyre rolls from the twelfth to the fourteenth centuries, found at JUST 1 and Curia Regis rolls at KB 26. The *eyre* was a circuit court, established from 1176, and the curia Regis ('the court of the King') was either the court at which the king actually presided, or before the *justiciar* – his representative.

A TIMELINE OF MAJOR EVENTS
Criminal Law and major influential events

1066 Norman Conquest

1086 The compilation of the Domesday Book

1135-1154 The reign of King Stephen: anarchy and disorder.

1166 Assize of Clarendon made the use of twelve 'legal' men from each hundred District responsible for presenting crimes they knew of.

1196 William Fitz Osbert, the first man to be hanged at Tyburn (now Marble Arch)

1215 Magna Carta created and signed by King John – among other rights, it protected subjects from arbitrary arrest and imprisonment.

1219 Trial by ordeal abolished

1234 The curia Regis divided and the King's Bench court established: this was the major Criminal court in the land.

1275 The Statute of Westminster: an attempt to curtail legal abuses in the criminal Justice system

1283 The Statute of Winchester –an attempt to codify the law.

1310-1316 General famine in England

1348 The Black Death (the plague) decimates the land

1351 Treason Act- the crime of 'compassing or imagining the King's death' Or 'levying war against the King in his realm.'

1361 Justices of the Peace formally created

The officials

Sheriff (shire-reeve) The chief officer of the crown in a county. He had the Power to select a jury and so make sure that he had the conviction he wanted. The Sheriff of Nottingham' in The Robin Hood stories was probably William de Brewere, Not really a sheriff, but an 'enforcer' for King John.

Justice of the peace A person appointed by the crown to be the person in a designated area who keeps the peace

Constable Before the professional police forces (after 1829) the constable was the man in each locality who had to supervise and enforce all kinds of laws and regulations.

THE TUDOR PERIOD

The years between the accession of Henry VII after the battle of Bosworth Field in 1485 and the death of Elizabeth I in 1603 marked all kinds of significant advances and changes in the criminal law. To understand these, and to grasp the mindset of the Tudors, a helpful framework to use is that of three areas of the criminal justice system: the central governmental consolidation of power and the acceleration of treason laws; the assize system in the 'circuits' across the shires, and the manorial and church courts.

The sixteenth century was a time of turmoil and potential anarchy from the parish level of what are know as petty sessions up to the Court of Star Chamber which dealt with serious crime. Having said that, serious crimes throughout the Tudor years and into the Stuart century could still sometimes he handled by quarter sessions, where criminals stood in front of the justices of the peace. But generally, the system worked with these three contexts and functions.

INSECURITY AND RELIGIOUS CONFLICT

If we start with the larger picture, then the court system and the legal process become clearer. From the beginning, the Tudors faced threats to their power from all quarters. Henry VII had to cope with pretenders to the throne, the result of the turmoil and confusion of the Wars of the Roses and the uncertainties of the right to accession of the first Tudor. Then his son, Henry VIII had a constant interlay of power games with the Holy See of the Pope and the concept of a European Christendom was eroded by nationalistic ambitions. Henry VIII broke with Rome and the Protestant Reformation meant that as the following monarchs succeeded, there were sways from Catholic to Protestant ideologies, and mass executions were a part of the suppression of religious practice.

There was a threat from Catholic Europe, coming to a head with the Spanish Armada of 1588, but there were also rebellions from within the commonwealth of the land: in 1536 The Pilgrimage of Grace, centred on Yorkshire and Lincolnshire originally, and the 1569 rebellion of the northern Catholic lords were the most significant uprisings, to say nothing of the various plots associated with Mary Queen of Scots and against Elizabeth by various factions as she continued in power without a heir.

PARISHES AND COURTS

All this is the story of major political upheaval, but in the counties and boroughs the criminal law went on, at local and regional level. The principal statutes that percolated down to roots level included The Act of Supremacy of 1534 and the following Act of Six Articles illustrate the repressive regime of the Tudor state. These made it a capital offence to deny the doctrine of transubstantiation. The 1559 Act of Supremacy abolished the power of the Pope in England. Many of the top-level crimes related to religious belief, and the executions at Smithfield were frequent. Torture was used, and execution often involved the horrors of hanging, drawing and quartering. But for everyday crime, the justices of the peace were the key positions in the law.

The assize courts continued to be the main arm of the King's justice system; the travelling justices rode over the network of the six circuits, twice a year (in summer and winter) and their duties were summed up in their power of 'oyer and terminer' and 'gaol delivery.' The first meant that they had to try and decide on the cases before then, and the latter that they had to 'empty the gaols' and hear all cases for which the poor unfortunates in the local gaols had been waiting for, in some cases for months.

The quarter sessions were run by the justices of the peace, and they were the first court to hear most of the trials in the county or borough, with the exception of matters heard at church courts. At the heart of this was the parish, and in the first part of this period they dealt with so much business that it became necessary to lighten the burden and petty session became more widespread. Much of the business at Quarter sessions was taken up with issues of bastardy, assaults, public disorder and beggars. The Tudors had to try to initiate a more workable poor law provision, such was the scale of the problems of poverty and vagrancy. A cursory glance at Shakespeare's plays shows the prevalence of beggars, wandering rogues and sellers of small items. If people wandered from their parish, they created problems.

Workhouses for the poor and houses of correction were products of the Tudor period; in 1576 and an Act was passed to provide 'houses of correction' in every county, and in 1597 'an Act for erecting hospitals and Working Houses for the Poor' was passed. As historian Christopher Hibbert wrote:

' . . . by the middle of the sixteenth century many men were mutilated and some were hanged for little worse than idleness.'

MANORIAL COURTS

One of the most fruitful ways to understand local justice provision in this period is to look at manorial records. The manors still had their own courts, dealing with local affairs: there were two kinds: the court baron and the court leet. The court baron was restricted to the business regarding the property and transactions of the lord of the manor, whereas the court leet was responsible for dealing with all kinds of minor offences.

A court leet might deal with such matters as piles of rubbish left on the highway, or drunkenness; with squabbles and with the pay of constables in the manor. Some of these have been printed with notes and explanations, notably by the Chetham Society www.chethams.org.uk/Chetham_Society.

To understand the scale of crime dealt with in manorial courts, reference can be made to J. A. Sharpe's example of the Lancashire manor of Prescott between 1615 and 1660. He notes that in that period, '1,252 inhabitants of the manor were presented for assault before the leet.'

*

WHERE TO FIND RECORDS

Assize Courts

From around 1559 the assize records begin to be available. The National Archives lists available material by county from 1559, and these include records in Wales also. Start at ASSI 5 and then at the county series from ASSI 6. The Palatinate Courts of Durham, Cheshire and Lancaster are also included here.

Quarter Sessions These are at county record offices in most cases. But some have been Printed in scholarly series, such as the West Riding Quarter Sessions Published by the Yorkshire Archaeological Society.

Manorial Courts TNA has a Manorial Documents Register. At local record offices there will be records, but they will be in Latin in this period. Regional Record Societies often produce these with transcripts or summaries in Book form. Court leet records are sometimes included in these.

Star Chamber These are at TNA, for the years 1485-1642, found at STAC 1 to STAC 9

OFFICIALS IN THE TUDOR CRIMINAL JUSTICE SYSTEM

Lord Lieutenant These were appointed after 1550, and were noblemen, having the highest status in the administration of the law in their county

Sheriff He administered the local government of the county. He was Responsible for arresting criminals and keeping them in Custody. From 1504, he could be fined if he was not up to these duties.

Justice of the Peace The local magistrate on the bench, unpaid. He was the 'workhorse' at the heart of local justice.

Constable The parish officer – appointed at petty sessions or leets to deal with minor parish matters and to control the 'watch and ward' (*watch*-night patrol/ *ward*- day patrol)

PUNISHMENT

The Tudor attitude to punishment was severe, and through modern eyes, completely barbaric. At local level, there was a stress on shaming punishments such as placing people in the stocks and pillory, or even branding miscreants. A so-called 'sturdy beggar' over the age of fourteen could be 'grievously whipped and burned through the gristle of the right ear with a hot iron with a compass of one inch.' In cases of serious felony and a death penalty, a woman could be burned for the murder of a husband, whereas the husband who killed a wife would be hanged. The reason was that a woman committed 'petty treason' and the husband murder.

For crimes of high treason, a death familiar today through the portrayals of execution scenes in popular films and television serials on the sixteenth century, the killings were often horribly cruel, as in the case of a man who denied the holiness of relics. He was 'hanged in chains, by the middle and arm-holes... and under the gallows was made a fire, and he was consumed and burnt to death.'

TIMELINE OF MAJOR LEGISLATION AND REBELLIONS
1485 Court of Star Chamber established
1534 and 1559 ACTS OF SUPREMACY
1534 Treason Act
1536 The Pilgrimage of Grace
1547-9 The Western Rebellion

1553-4 Thomas Wyatt's conspiracy and rebellion
1569 The Northern rebellion
1576 Houses of Correction established
1597 'Working Houses for the Poor' created
1603 Poor Law Act

THE SEVENTEENTH CENTURY

In the years between the death of Queen Elizabeth I in 1603 and the accession of Queen Anne in 1702 the story of crime in England is crowded with high profile treason trials, violent rebellions and above all, the execution of King Charles I in 1649. That judicial killing opens up the debate about who was 'criminal' in that terrible event. It was a brutal, vicious century with a Civil War in the middle years in which brother fought brother on the battlefield and which saw the horrendous persecutions of witches in many areas of the land.

But the famous and infamous were not the only victims of the repressive criminal law: in the year that King Charles was beheaded, 23 men and one woman were hanged at Tyburn (which was where Marble Arch now stands) for burglary and robbery. It took eight carts to carry the felons to their date with the rope, and the event was the largest number of criminals ever hanged in one session in Britain. The hangings were excuses for heavy drinking and violence in the London mob.

REPRESSION AND SAVAGERY

It is in the seventeenth century that the beginnings of the proliferation of capital crimes began, and these were applied to several areas of life. In the Game Laws of 1684, for instance, the taking of game by anyone except the owner of the land was forbidden. A series of statutes established this. Only people who owned a freehold estate worth £100 a year, or a leasehold of £150 a year were allowed to take game. Poaching had always been looked upon, in rural communities, as a 'social crime' – meaning that there was a certain degree of tolerance in that often the killing of rabbits or birds might hold off starvation for a poor man's family. The thinking behind these tough laws may be seen in the 1671 Coventry Act, which made it a criminal offence to loiter with intent to maim. Sir John Coventry had been attacked and had his nose slit in London, and that prompted the legislation.

In terms of the political life, serious offences were punished by hanging, drawing and quartering. In October 1660 two unfortunates, John Cooke and Hugh Peters, suffered this fate: 'When Mr Cook was cut down and brought to be quartered, one they called Colonel Turner called that he might see it…. The hangman came to him smeared in blood.' He had done the unenviable task of cutting the bodies of the men in quarters while they still breathed.

The 'Bloody Assizes' of 1685 typify this savage reprisal for treason and rebellion: after the Monmouth rebellion in June of that year, in which the Duke of Monmouth had landed with an army at Lyme in Dorset, gathered a large force and proclaimed himself king, there was a brutal reprisal waiting him after his defeat. The so-called Bloody Assizes sentenced over 300 people to death. One of the victims was seventy year old Lady Alice Lyle who was beheaded for treason at Winchester, convicted for harbouring traitors.

Opposing the sovereigns was always courageous and often suicidal. The great parliamentarian, John Hampden, opposed Charles the 1sts demands for ship money and was imprisoned in 1627, for fighting the notion of a 'forced loan.' The great judge Sir Richard Hutton also refused to accept the legality of the Ship Money extortion by the King, but he escaped any punishment.

EVERYDAY LAW

But for most people in Britain at this time, the common offences of daily life were dealt with in quarter sessions before magistrates, and at church or manorial courts. The records for these are primarily in Latin in this period – until 1733. But the records are not necessarily all in the county archives. Many have been printed and translated. For instance, the Yorkshire Archaeological Society printed the quarter sessions for the West Riding in parts of this century, and these give a valuable insight into the process of law.

In 1637, for instance, Sir Francis Wortley and other dignitaries sat in judgement at Doncaster on a variety of accused persons. Katherine Booth had broken into a house and stolen a chest of goods; one man had stolen a bible and another had robbed someone of a petticoat and a 'peck of oatmeal.' At the end of the session, we had this situation:

'They were led to the bar by the sheriff and asked what they could say forthemselves, why they should not have judgement of death according to the Law for the felonies aforesaid whereof they were convicted. They severally said that they were clerks and prayed for the benefit of clergy...'

This was the one way to escape hanging up until the nineteenth century. If a person could recite the 'neck verse' – the opening of the 51st psalm, they would not hang, but have their thumb branded instead. The benefit of clergy could only be given once.

But there was always the communal, public retribution for what might be called 'moral crimes.' In 1619 there was a case in the Court of Star Chamber in which William and Margaret Cripple of Burton-on-Trent prosecuted residents there: they had been attacked by a mob for 'sexual incontinency.' Not only were they dragged through the streets, they were then put in the stocks and people 'pissed on their heads.'

The *court leets* (from Anglo-Saxon *'laeth'* – a county)and manorial courts give a similar picture: a large amount of criminal business passed through these institutions and the majority are such matters as drunkenness, public nuisances, payment of dues, licences to retail goods and maintaining parish responsibilities.

HIGHWAYMEN

The word 'highwayman' now suggests a glamorous 'gentleman of the road' but in reality these men were nasty, unprincipled villains who preyed on the defenceless. In the classic 'true crime' works of The Newgate Calendar and in the sessions accounts of the Old Bailey, for instance, the name of Claude Duval is prominent. He was a footman to the wealthy turned robber; Duval even robbed the master of horse of King Charles II in his reign of terror on the open road. He was finally caught in a drunken state in Chandos Street, London and hanged at Tyburn. He was just twenty-seven years old

Captain James Hind, born in Chipping Norton in 1619, was another highway robber – the typical 'gentleman highwayman' of popular tales and ballads. He was supposed to rob only Roundheads, and some say he even robbed Oliver Cromwell; he was a celebrated Royalist and at one time, before robbing people, he said, 'I neither fear you nor any king-killing villain alive. I now have as much power over you as you had lately over the King.' He was executed for treason in 1652.

AN AGE OF WITCH-FINDING

The seventeenth century was undoubtedly the era of witch prosecutions. In August, 1682 the Bideford witches were hanged at Heavitree gallows in Exeter, and then Alice Molland in 1684 – the latter being the last known execution of a witch in England: in 1736 witchcraft was no longer a capital offence. But the century began with witch trials. In 1619 there was the case of the Belvoir Witches: two 'goodwives' called Margaret and Phillipa Flower were accused by locals of witchcraft, supposedly guilty of manipulating the children of the Earl of Rutland. They were tried and hanged at Lincoln. The most famous case was that of the Lancashire Witches in 1612. A man called John Law gave evidence that he had been bewitched : *'He deposeth and saith that about eighteenth of March last past... he met with Alizon Device, who was very earnest for pinnes, but he would give her none; whereupon she seemed to be very angry, and when he was past her he fell down lame in great extremity...'*

By the end of the century, thankfully this kind of accusation and trial was declining. Sir John Holt, who was Lord Chief Justice in 1689, dismissed every witchcraft case that came before him. The last conviction was in 1712, and the woman in question, Jane Wenham, was pardoned.

The Neck Verse:
Have mercy upon me, o God, according to thy loving kindness: according to the multitude of Thy tender mercies blot out my transgressions.'

An old verse explains the origins:
'If a clerk had been taken /for stealing of bacon
For burglary, murder or rape/ if he could but rehearse
(well prompt) his neck verse/ he never could fail to escape.'

Timeline
1612 Trials of the Lancashire Witches
1637-38 John Hampden opposes the King's 'Ship Money'
1642-1651 The Civil Wars
1649 Execution of Charles I
1680s-1690's Widespread riots: 1693 Food riots in Severn Valley; 1695 election riots at Oxford; 1697 anti-enclosure riots at Epworth in Lincolnshire.
1671 The Coventry Act
1684 Game Laws
1685 Monmouth Rebellion and the 'Bloody Assizes.'
1699 Shoplifting Act: Stealing of goods valued at five shillings and over was a capital crime.

Where to find the records

Assize court indictments These were in Latin until 1733. Start with criminal registers at TNA HO 27, then consult TNA Assizes: Key to Criminal Trials 1559-1971

Assize court records for 1559-1971 are accessed after finding out where a trial took place, using the criminal registers at HO140. From 1613 the series is at ASSI 45. The records were in Latin up to 1733.

Judges reports at TNA start at 1783. See HO 47 for 1783-1830.

Transportation: TNA series T1 and in T53 for America, and HO 11 for Australia (1787-1867)

Prison: County Record Offices will have quarter sessions material and calendars of prisoners.

Police: see Stephen Wade *Tracing Your Police Ancestors* (Pen and Sword 2009)

Comprehensive Reference for all areas: David T. Hawkings, *Criminal Ancestors* (Sutton, 2009)

Old Bailey Sessions Papers: These cover the years 1674 to 1913 and are searchable online. In addition to the trial records, there are accounts by 'ordinaries' (gaolers) from Newgate between 1679 and 1772.

Church Court records are many and varied; manorial court leets will be at county record offices. But there are indexes and these prove very useful, such as the *Index of Cases in the Records of the Court of Arches at Lambeth Palace 1660-1913* by Jane Houston (1972)

Also, the Borthwick Institute at York has similar indexes for the Diocese of York. See www.york.ac.uk/inst/bihr

Court of King's Bench (known as the Upper Bench 1649-1660)The index at KB10 is the place to start.

Check also in the new edition of *Criminal Ancestors* by David T Hawkings (History Press, 2010)
Finding defendants in the regions: look at INDI/6678-6679

THE EIGHTEENTH CENTURY AND REGENCY

When we think of the popular images of crime in the 'long' eighteenth century (c.1700-1837), the aspects of the period that come to mind are probably Dick Turpin the highwayman, smugglers and horrible hangings at Tyburn. These kinds of images stem partly from popular culture – mainly film and novels – but also from countless illustrations in books, magazines and documentaries depicting the sheer vicious lawlessness of that century.

But in fact the most dominant criminal events of the years were arguably the Jacobite insurrections of 1715 and 1745; the riots and disorder which occurred for all kinds of reasons; offences against the Game Laws, transportation, the birth of professional police, and sedition. Although there was a high level of homicide and crimes against the person in that period, and a series of repressive Murder Acts, what takes the limelight for crime history is the political narrative.

If we look at some of the major legislation of the time, we find a hugely influential statute in 1715, The Riot Act; then the 1718 Transportation Act, which gave courts the power to transport some felons to the American colonies; the Black Act of 1723 which added a large number of offences to the established 'Bloody Code' discussed in the last Chronicle; and finally the various acts against sedition and radicalism in the Regency years, all aimed at preventing the open or secret dissemination of radical political ideas during and after the French Revolution of 1789.

VIOLENCE AND FEAR

The period is marked at every level of crime as one of horrendous repression and punishment. The British citizen was under threat from robbers and muggers at all times in the towns and of course in London, but nocturnal fears were severe: after all, a man and his household were only protected by the 'watch and ward' officers who were generally ineffective. At the end of the is period, we have Sir Robert Peel's Police Act of 1829, and much earlier there were the Bow Street magistrates and 'Runners' in London, but for the country in general, there were perils everywhere. In 1728, for instance, John Byrom had a meeting with a highwayman. He wrote a letter to his wife describing this: '… about half a mile or less off Epping, a highwayman in a red rug upon a black horse came out of the bushes up to the coach, and presenting pistol, first at the coachman and then at the corporation within, with a volley of oaths demanded our money…' Shots were fired and the passengers parted with cash and silver. But the robberies went on daily: copies of *The Gentleman's Magazine* and *The Annual Register* are peppered with reports of nasty and brutal attacks, dreadful murders and brutal hangings.

The number of capital crimes gradually increased throughout this period, until by the 1820s there were over two hundred such offences. Judges on the assize circuits found a procession of culprits standing before them –often very young – who could technically be hanged for what we would think of as small thefts. For a 'grand larceny' the sentence was death, so courts and the Bench often humanely changed the value of stolen goods so that they would be related to simple larceny.

A typical crime of this time, when the country was still predominantly rural, is this from Lincolnshire in 1760, when Mary baker prosecuted a shepherd of Willoughton for assault: he was in court for 'violently beating and abusing her with his foot and for striking her with his fist, and punching her down and striking her head against a wall...'

RIOT AND DISORDER
But it was also a time when there was trouble in the streets, in the country, and in the new mills. In 1769 attacks on mills were included in the offences subject to the Riot Act, and later in this period, political radicalism brought extreme measures. In 1799 and 1800 the Combination Act outlawed meetings in streets of more than six people; after the Luddite troubles of 1812, when machine-wreckers (named after a fabled figure called Ned Ludd) set about destroying mills in Yorkshire, a new offence of administering an illegal oath was created, so that more felons could be hanged or sent to Van Dieman's Land (Tasmania).

Some riots were not merely in response to the price of corn; the Gordon Riots of 1780 in London, lasted for six days, after Lord George Gordon presented a petition to parliament against Catholic rights. People were killed and in the end 135 people stood trial. Riots were linked to sedition, and in 1792 there was a proclamation against seditious publications, and even the great statesman Thomas Paine was tried (*in absentia*) and convicted of sedition.

Another aspect of this was mutiny. The Napoleonic Wars led to numerous side-effects, and mutiny was one of these: in 1797 after a dangerous mutiny at the Nore men were tried and hanged, and in 1819 the assembly of people for political reasons received its most brutal response from the authorities in these years when the Peterloo Massacre occurred in Manchester: here, the famous speaker Henry 'Orator' Hunt addressed an immense crowd, gathered peaceably, but the yeomanry intervened and in that bloody encounter, eleven people were killed and many more wounded.

But riots could break out for all kinds of reasons: there were food riots in Cornwall in 1727; anti-enclosure riots in the Forest of Dean in 1735, and election riots in several places in 1734. Crowds gathered to destroy turnpikes in Bristol in 1749 and in 1751 two women suspected of being witches were murdered by a crowd in Tring.

One report in the press from 1755 gives some idea of the trouble that was often experienced:

' May, Selby, Yorks. The bellman made proclamation for the inhabitants to bring their hatchets and axes at 12 o'clock that night to cut down the turnpike erected by Act of Parliament. Accordingly, the great gate with five rails was totally destroyed by some riotous persons...'

TYBURN 'THEATRE'

The abiding image of the criminal justice system in the Georgian years is one of trials at the Old Bailey and hangings at Newgate or Tyburn, accompanied by huge crowds. Of course, there is some truth in this, but we have to recall that many were sentenced to die but also many were reprieved. Between 1814 and 1834 for instance, almost five thousand people were sentenced to hang for burglary, but only 233 hanged. But nevertheless, the hangman was busy. After the Murder Act of 1752, a felon was to be hanged within just 48 hours of sentencing. Until 1760, a 'triple tree' was used at Tyburn, a wooden frame with three sides, so that several people could be hanged at once; this was replaced by a portable gallows in that year. Hangings at Tyburn (now Marble Arch) ended in 1783, and from December of that year executions took place at Newgate. The so-called 'new drop' there was the scene of a multiple hanging in 1783, when nine men and a woman were on the scaffold.

Until 1784, a wife murdering a husband would be burned at the stake rather than hanged, as her crime was petty treason, not murder. In that year Mary Bailey was the last to suffer that horrible fate although it was common practice for the hangman, for a small bribe, to strangle the women before she was tied to the stake. For treason, a person could be hanged, drawn and quartered until 1820, when the famous Cato Street conspirators suffered that fate.

TRANSPORTATION AND PRISONS

After the loss of the American colonies, transportation was to Australia, beginning in 1787. Between 1815 and 1829, around 12,000 convicts were transported to Australia. The process involved a period in a specific colony, and then work on probation teams, so that for instance, convicts in Tasmania would at times be allocated to gaols in Richmond and work in teams to do public works, such as bridge-building.

Prisons in this period were seriously dangerous places to be. The assize system meant that prisoners on remand awaiting trial had to languish in disease-ridden cells until the judges arrived on the circuit to clear the gaols. Local gaols and houses of correction were, however, the subject of a study and survey by the great prison reformer John Howard. His book, *The State of the Prisons* (1777) was the first step in the movement towards making prisons more humane and open to some notions of rehabilitation and reform rather than mere punishment and hard work in a 'silent system.'

The eighteenth century gaol, was however, a mix of factory, punishment block and going concern – in the sense that wealthier inmates could still have communication with the community outside, buying food and drink and having visitors. Debtors lived alongside hardened criminals: John Wesley's father, Samuel, was a debtor in Lincoln gaol.

POLICE

This period saw the gradual emergence of the professional police. The brothers Henry and John Fielding had developed a reasonably successful London police force in the mid century, though its scope was very limited. Then in 1800 there was a police office established at Wapping, and in 1829 the Metropolitan Police Act came into force, forming a paid, full-time police force which operated within a radius of about seven miles of London. Provincial forces were to come later.

*

Timeline
CRIMINAL LAW AND MAJOR INFLUENTIAL EVENTS

1715	The Riot Act
1718	Transportation Act
1745	The Jacobite Insurrection: 'Bonny Prince Charlie'
1753	'The Bow Street constable' established
1780	The Gordon Riots
1789	The French Revolution
1799-1800	Combination Acts
1812	Luddite attacks
1819	The Peterloo Massacre in Manchester
1829	Metropolitan Police Act

The Victorian Age 1837-1901

When Queen Victoria ascended the throne in 1837 there had been significant developments in the criminal justice system, largely thanks to Sir Robert Peel. It would not be stretching the facts too much to say that there had been a revolution in crime and punishment in the ten years before she became queen. Peel had established the first truly professional police force in 1829, and his Gaol Acts had gone some way to providing regulation and inspection in regional gaols and houses of correction.

The last years of the Regency experienced the widespread fear of political and social change impacting on popular feeling and radicalism had brought massive and often terrifying disorder. But in spite of the riots, sedition and arson of the tough first years of the 1830s, there had been important developments, mainly the abolition of a large number of capital offences. Although the retribution of the courts against criminals was still swift and savage, there were signs that more humane attitudes were coming through. By 1837 only sixteen crimes had capital sentences.

By the end of the century, white collar crime had increased markedly, and serious crime against the person was less prominent, though Britain was still a society with a massive drink problem, and violence was never far away, particularly in the new towns, where long hours of hard work and deprivation combined with drunkenness to create an underclass of so-called 'habitual criminals ' who crowded the police courts and magistrates' courts.

A Nation Divided

One notable feature of crime in the first half of Victoria's reign was the acceleration of the class divisions: the rich and poor were sharply aware of their differences. In Manchester in the 1840s for instance, as the novelist Elizabeth Gaskell describes in *North and South* the villas of the new rich, the masters of industry, were in one area of the city, strictly separate from the urban ghetto in which the mill workers lived in basement slums, struggling with all the problems poverty, poor public health and low wages bring.

In the 1840s, the writers were so aware of what came to be called 'The Two Englands' that it comes as no surprise that the criminal courts were busy. Theft and assault come often from desperation – men stealing to feed the family or women entering the sex trade in order to earn some extra cash.

The Reform Act of 1832 had been a huge disappointment to many of the lower middle class, as so many features of the corrupt and divisive political structures of the land had left them without the vote and other rights. Trade unions were illegal and men were transported or imprisoned for working towards establishing unions. By 1851, the artisan class were beginning to creep into some kind of recognition in a corporate sense, with the creation of the Amalgamated Society of Engineers. But for the working man and woman, most of the Victorian period was one of very long working hours, poor pay and limited social support. The workhouse was a constant threat and was seen as little better than a prison.

The Police Reforms
Peel's Metropolitan Police were on the streets by 1829 and by the 1850s, regional forces were being created. There was resistance and suspicion from the start. People thought that a general and professional force would create a police state and they were seen as quasi-military, being compared to the repressive regime in France. After the establishment of the detective force in 1842, these fears were reinforced for many. But the fact is that the new police gradually learned and adapted, so that by the last decades of the century they had created specialists to deal with such matters as anarchists, Irish Fenians and large-scale fraud. The C.I.D. was created in 1874, and by the end of the century the top police officers were involved in early measures towards national security.

The 1839 County Police Act gave boroughs the option of starting a constabulary, if the justices wanted to levy a rate for that purpose, and in 1856 the County and Borough Police Act made it compulsory for all counties in England and Wales to establish police forces. In the year of Victoria's accession, the first black police officer was appointed – John Kent, who joined the Carlisle police force.

Tough Punishment

The prison system and the criminal courts still maintained a central ideology of harsh repression and a very narrow, regulatory practice in terms of allowing more of the human element into the justice system. For instance, there was no probation service until 1907, though the police court missionaries did their best to keep offenders out of a recidivist life.

The first model prison was constructed at Millbank. A separate system for men and women was established. A study of the prison plans, published in parliamentary papers, for this period shows the very specific and purpose-built accommodation for different classes and sexes. By 1877 the prisons were effectively nationalised and many old local houses of correction were phased out.

Transportation continued until 1853 to Tasmania (Van Dieman's Land) and in the same year the Penal Servitude Act made the idea of punishment itself, the removal of individual freedom, the core of the penal system. By the 1860s, the application of a ticket of leave process, whereby convicts could be released early for good behaviour, led to epidemics of assaults, notably the garrotting reign of terror in 1863-5 in which gangs preyed on the rich in city streets. The response was, naturally, a call for tougher punishments and more use of the whip and birch. In 1867 transportation ended completely.

By 1861 the number of capital offences was reduced to just four: murder, arson in a royal dockyard, high treason and piracy. In that year the last execution for attempted murder took place when Martin Doyle was hanged in Chester. But public hangings continued until 1868, and up to that time the hanging of a felon was still a public spectacle on a massive scale. In popular culture, murder and hanging were placed in all kinds of narratives and entertainments. Charles Dickens reported that pictures of murderers were in the print shops, and he wrote that 'high prices were offered for murderer's clothes at Newgate.'

Hangings in a 'Civilised' Society

When we consider the surface features of the Victorian world – polite social events, dances, protocol and good manners – it is easy to forget how barbaric were the acts done in the name of civilisation. It may have been a Christian society, but after the 1857 Indian Mutiny, for instance, some of the leaders of the rebellion were 'Fired at cannon' – meaning that they were strapped across the barrel of a cannon and then obliterated.

The same attitudes lay behind the public hangings. In 1840 the murder of Lord William Russell was one of the most notorious Victorian cases: this was because he had been killed by a servant. Until 1829, this offence was classified as Petty Treason, and the killer would have been burned at the stake, not hanged. In this case, the killer, Francois Courvoisier, was hanged. At his trial, crowds pushed and shoved to find a seat at the Old Bailey; the judge presiding was short of room and the name of Courvoisier was on everyone's lips in the taverns and coffee-houses.

At the hanging there were 40,000 spectators. The novelist, William Thackeray was in the crowd, and he wrote afterwards:

'I came away from Snow Hill that morning with a disgust for murder, but it was for the murder I saw done.... So salutary has the impression of the butchery been upon me that I can see Mr. Ketch at this moment, with an easy air, taking the rope from his pocket...'

The hangman was William Calcraft, a celebrity at the time. He had to let the body hang for an hour before he could cut it down. The body was then buried within the walls of Newgate. But just a month after, Courvoisier was seen in waxwork effigy at Madame Tussaud's.

Courts and Trials

There was a massive amount of legislation throughout the Victorian years affecting the criminal courts. As the century wore on, the police courts took on most of the everyday work, as there was such a high level of petty crime that the magistrates could not cope. But for more serious crime, the assizes and the Old Bailey were the arenas where serious crime would be affected by various developments. In the matter of defences for instances, both insanity and provocation were extremely hard to prove. The 1843 McNaghten Rules were the main guidance for barristers and judges: Daniel McNaghten at that time tried to murder Sir Robert Peel but was judged to be insane. He was 'labouring under such defect of reason, from disease of the mind, as not to know the nature and the quality of the act he/she was doing.'

For provocation and insanity, there were hundreds of homicide cases in which the killer (usually a husband) tried to claim either 'temporary insanity' because of drunkenness, or provocation because the wife or woman in question was inconstant.

Imprisonment for debts under £20 was abolished in 1844, and in 1861, imprisonment for debt ended completely.

But amazingly, it was not until the 1890s that the accused could speak in court, and also there was no general court of criminal appeal until 1907. The only chance of a rethink about a criminal court sentence before the end of the century would have been the 'Crown cases Reserved' in which a judge would press the matter in a select group of learned colleagues.

Industrial Relations and Commercial Crime
With the Industrial Revolution and the widespread shift of labour to the new urban conurbations, and the large-scale immigration of workers needed for the new industries, crime came not only with the socials divisions and the 'haves and have-nots' but through industrial strife. In terms of industrial problems, the illegality of unions led to constant trouble when 'black-leg' labour was imported. The 1859 Molestation of Workmen Act tried to do something about this, but in 1866, the 'Sheffield Outrages' typified the lamentable results of union problems: non-union cutlery workers were attacked by their fellow workmen. In the following year the Master and Servant Act put some limitations on the mechanism for prosecuting strikers for breach of contract, but members could still face the law if they were thought to be 'aggravated cases.'

But trouble was always there, ready to erupt. Typical of this was the nine-week strike of cotton weavers in Lancashire in1878 in which there were confrontations in Preston and Blackburn, and then the celebrated London dockers' strike of 1889 in which the dockers won six pence an hour. In 1893 two people were killed at Featherstone when soldiers and strikers clashed at Acton Hall colliery.

There was an increase in white-collar crime in the second half of the century, and fraud, forgery and deception were often in the news and reported from the courts. Typical of this was what became the first 'true crime' story on film, when a clerk called Thomas Goudie forged cheques while working with the Bank of Liverpool. He was threatened by a racetrack gang to do this, but was found out and arrested, being given a sentence of ten years but died in gaol after serving six years. . Dramatic scenes from Goudie's story were filmed by local film-makers, Mitchell and Kenyon (see *The Lost World of Mitchell and Kenyon*, BBC DVD).

In the City of London, naturally, such crimes proliferated, and always did. But recent research has unearthed a number of little-known sources of material on forgery from the Bank of England, for instance. A cursory trawl through the London magistrates' courts and the Guildhall, Old Bailey sessions papers and assizes will show the escalation of fraudulent offences in these years. The Queen's reign began with trouble in the streets, social divisions and violent domestic crime, and ended with the dominance of counterfeiters, forgers and con-men stealing the headlines from the muggers and thieves.

*

Timeline of Important Legislation

1829   The Metropolitan Police Act. This created a London police force with full professional organisation

1839-1842 Chartist demonstrations and troubles: spies used by the Government

1843   The McNaghten Rules established for insanity pleas.

1856   County and Borough Police Act: all counties were forced to set up constabularies

1861   Capital offences reduced to just four. Imprisonment for debt abolished

1867   The end of transportation

1868   Public hangings abolished. The last public hanging (in England) takes place: Michael Barrett at Newgate

1873   Single High Court is created, replacing seven existing courts

1877   The Prison Act nationalises the prisons

1894   The 'Borstal' scheme first planned

Case Study
ANOTHER WIFE MURDER
Robert Nall 9 April, 1842
Nall had given his wife Mary years of sheer hell before they parted, and even then he would not leave her alone. His demands turned to frustration and then to violence and he was heard to say to her, 'Thou must prepare thyself for a coffin tomorrow morning for I mean to stick thee.' He took rather longer than he at first said, but later expressed his resolve again, saying he would have a free ride to York. But they were back together again two months later.

In late November, they spent a night together at the Hull Beer House in Sheffield's Wicker district. They then moved on to his sister's house and they were drunk; they persuaded her to let them stay, as they were drifting around until they could live with her

mother – something that was not likely to happen. Nall's sister returned from a visit to find that her brother was uneasy and in a strange mood. Later, when she was even more worried, she brought a watchman and the two of them found Nall in bed with Mary – but the woman was dead. She was covered in blood, and Nall produced a knife, which he gave to the watchman.

The watchman, Macklin, made a careful note of what Nall said after that. The man said that he had tried to stab himself and to hang himself, but had not had the resolve to do it. When questioned further, Nall told a story of how, when they were together and drunk, they had argued and Mary had said that she would ,'Go with who she liked when she liked.' That provoked him into stabbing her. He had taken her life and then lay with her as she died, waiting for retribution. At the inquest, the coroner said that he had never known a more deliberate act of murder, and Nall was sent to York for that 'free ride' he had spoken of.

Mr Justice Coltman heard that familiar plea of insanity yet again; the argument was that an industrial accident which had happened to Nall some time before had left him with a mental derangement. A surgeon gave supporting evidence to that, but to no avail. There was no possibility of manslaughter and no provocation. After half an hour, the jury found Nall guilty of murder but did recommend mercy, but nothing changed the judge's mind that Nall should hang. He said to Nall, ' The state of mind you were in was not such as legally to extenuate your crime. You were responsible for your acts…. And you must suffer for it.' He was hanged with another wife-killer, Jonathan Taylor.

The twentieth century is surely remembered in the history of crimes for arguably the most sickening and extreme of all offences: the war crimes of the Nazis and the Holocaust. But that statement would be rivalled by the genocides in Russia, Vietnam and elsewhere. If we have to keep the focus on Britain, then certain landmark moments steal the light of historical enquiry. The century began with the street battles against anarchists and ended with some large-scale 'white collar' frauds and new dimensions of mass and serial murder. In contrast, in 1907 the Court of Criminal Appeal made appeals possible for almost anyone, the case brought by lawyers. But in between, the spin-off crime of two world wars and massive urban development give us the spine of the criminal narrative of the last century.

Edwardian Horrors

The years between c.1900 and 1920 saw some astonishing developments in crime-fighting, such as the use of fingerprinting and specialist police squads. The Great War years also saw the first great achievements of the fledgling MI5 in the war against spies on the domestic front. But what steals the headlines is murder. Perhaps the most notorious at the time was that of the murder of Cora Crippen by her husband, Dr Hawley Crippen. Recent work in mitochondrial DNA has cast doubt on exactly whose body lies in the cellar of 39 Hilltop Crescent, but at the time Crippen was sentenced with her murder, after the first arrest brought about by the use of the 'wireless' as Crippen and his mistress Ethel le Neve were spotted on board the SS Montrose by the alert captain. Crippen was hanged at Pentonville in November, 1910 and Ethel emigrated to Australia.

But there were other fears in the streets as well the terror of murder; there were anarchists about in London, and in the famous Siege of Sidney Street in 1911, some members of a gang of Latvian political refugees who had been involved in the Houndsditch murders of 1909 in which a child and a police officer had been shot dead and seventeen other people injured. At number 11, Exchange Buildings a gang led by George Garstein killed two police sergeants and a constable. Winston Churchill himself (the Home Secretary) joined the troops and detectives who finally trapped the killers, and the building was destroyed, along with the gang, in a fire. It is one of the few crimes of this kind for which we have photographic records, and there are even postcards available showing the dramatic action in the streets.

Everyday Killings and Law Reform
After the Great War, the records show an increase in domestic murder: the usual event was the strangling or throat-slitting of the female victim, often by her husband or lover. The war had left thousands of men mentally scarred, and what was called neurasthenia or 'shell shock' was often treated simply with rest rather than direct therapy. Large numbers of ex-servicemen were destined for the scaffold for murder in this kind of situation, like John Crossland, who had fought at Mons where he was wounded; his marriage failed on being demobbed and eventually he battered to death his wife Ellen in Blackburn in May, 1919.

But as murder was still a large-scale social problem and the hangman was kept busy until 1964 in England, there were important reforms in criminal law as the century went on. In 1922, for instance, infanticide was made a version of manslaughter rather than murder, and in 1938 the Infanticide Act dealt with the medical factors, as there was more understanding on post-natal psychosis, and although there were some executions of women – notably Ethel Major at Hull in 1934 and Ruth Ellis in 1955 – capital punishment reforms were gradually carried through.

The Homicide Act of 1957 made clear some guidelines on diminished responsibility. The line of thought was that if a person was suffering from such abnormality of mind when the homicide was committed that his or her judgement was impaired, then the conviction would be for manslaughter.

Yet, amazingly, the Witchcraft Act was not abolished until 1951, and this statute had been used in the prosecution of Helen Duncan in March 1944, after this psychic medium claimed to know about the sinking of HMS Barham before the news was released by the government. An apparition of a sailor appeared at her séance and had the ship's name on his hat when he reputedly said, 'Sorry, sweetheart, my ship sank in the Mediterranean.. I've crossed over to the other side.' Duncan served a spell in gaol for that 'breach of national security' and was the last woman tried under the Witchcraft Act in England.

Another very significant date in this context was 1961 when the Suicide Act abrogated the act as a criminal offence; but complicity in a suicide carried a prison term of fourteen years, and so some notable cases of suicide pacts meant that serious crimes were committed.

The last hangings in this country took place in 1964 when Peter Allen and Gwynne Evans were hanged in April, 1964, on the same day, one in Manchester and one in Liverpool. Then in 1965 the Murder (Abolition of Death Penalty) Act was passed, ending capital punishment for murder.

Gangs, Rackets and Spivs

The 1920s and the years of the second world war saw a notable increase in gangs and in black market rackets. The influence of Hollywood gangster movies may have been a factor in this, and there was glamour attached to stars of the underworld such as Al Capone and Dillinger. But there was nothing glamorous about the fights and killings between the London and provincial gangs who ran racetrack protection rackets and fought over their 'patch' with guns and knives.

The Sabini gang was started by Charles 'Darby' Sabini, a middleweight boxer who had dressed like a tramp and lived in a hovel, and he has been described by writer Dick Kirby as someone who 'dressed scruffily in hat and scarf and was painfully uneducated…. With his mouthful of gold teeth, he liked to portray himself as a simple peasant like Robin Hood….' Joe was one of his brothers, along with George, Fred and Harry boy. They were involved in protection rackets and often fell foul of the law. In some ways this established the pattern of later organisations such as the infamous Krays, Ronald and Reginald, who controlled the London underworld in the 1960s.

There was gang rivalry with the Krays too, of course: their main threat being the Richardson gang. In 1965 a full gang war began after a Richardson member called Cornell went too far with insults about Ronnie Kray. Ronnie shot Cornell dead, before several witnesses, but no-one wanted to tell the tale. Reggie followed suit, killing Jack 'The Hat' McVitie after luring him to a party.

But on a more everyday level, the middle years of the century saw all kinds of variations on theft and robbery, particularly after the second world war, because gangs were formed who had weapons left over from the war. The 1950s saw a flood of armed robberies, many on small shops and clubs or factories. There were also the spivs: the word spiv had been in use for decades before the 1940s, but that was the decade in which it became something in general use. A book called *The Other Half: The Autobiography of a Spiv* by John Worby was published in 1937 and that had an impact. The spiv was often only working for small amounts but was also a 'wide boy' –someone well aware of the criminal fraternity and open to offers and opportunities. In that way the word also began to be used of a fashion and an attitude to life.

The wartime black market was a massive influence on all the rackets and underworld scams of course, a typical example being the appropriation of parachute material to be made into ladies' underwear. As there was wartime rationing, then naturally the criminal class found ways of providing goods and materials in short supply – for a price. Forgery was a part of this too, with such items as ration books and coupons being forged.

Of course, the Great Train Robbery of 1963 in some ways towers above all of this: Bruce Reynolds and his gang of professional thieves who based themselves at a farm near a rail track and succeeded in breaking into a Royal Mail carriage and in 24 minutes stole over two and a half million pounds. This was split seventeen ways and each man had around £150,000.

The late twentieth century saw the increase in both numbers and intensity of the serial and mass killers, and lessons were learned by police after the notorious case of the Yorkshire Ripper who terrorised women in Yorkshire in between 1975 and 1981, killing at least nine victims. From that case came a number of prominent criminological advances, including mapping and the use of profiling more extensively.

In 1987 one of the first horrendous mass killings of modern times took place at Hungerford in Berkshire, when Michael Ryan shot and killed 16 people and wounded another fourteen. Some label this a 'spree ' killing, and like a serial killer, the spree or mass killer is an increasingly common phenomenon today.

The DNA Revolution

In 1984 Professor Alec Jeffreys at Leicester University discovered a way of studying and monitoring DNA sequences and so it became possible to individuate samples from crimes, locating the presence of the criminal with great certainty. Over the next twenty years DNA evidence became an accepted part of court evidence as well as of police detective work. Within the last year there have been four high-profile arrests with reference to crimes committed thirty years ago, made possible by more advances in DNA sampling.

The century began with the first conviction made possible by fingerprinting (in 1905) and ended with several arrests done with DNA science behind the police work.

Timeline

1905 The first convictions given on fingerprint evidence

1907 The court of criminal appeal established
1910 The arrest of Dr Crippen after the use of wireless to catch him
1910-1911 The Houndsditch Murders and the Siege of Sidney Street
1922 and 1938 Infanticide legislation shifting it from the murder category
1961 Suicide no longer a criminal offence
1963 The Great Train Robbery
1964 The last hangings in Britain.
1971 Crown Courts introduced
1975-1981 The reign of terror of the Yorkshire Ripper
1987 The Hungerford Massacre
1984 DNA sampling established. It took a long time for DNA evidence to be something that juries could understand, and it was a tough challenge for barristers to find ways to explain the technicalities in a meaningful way, and with an approach that would appeal to the court's common sense and level of understanding of arcane science.

Where to find the Records
County record offices have a variety of criminal records, but at TNA there are the assize records up to 1971 when the circuits were ended and the crown courts established.
David T Hawking's book *Criminal Ancestors* (History Press, 2010) has listings of locations regarding both prison records and assize records. Records after the 1950s are hard to access and Crown Courts records are variable in terms of accessibility, so Access to Archives (A2A) is a good place to start to see what is there.

For courts of appeal, there is a full printed series from 1907 to the present, published by Sweet and Maxwell and usually available in university libraries.

On the macabre side, for a full account of all twentieth century hangings see John J Eddleston, *The Encyclopaedia of Executions* (Blake, 2002)

Assize records: See TNA key for Criminal Trials 1559-1971 and Assizes, Welsh, 1831-1971. Click on 'assize records' at the TNA website
Old Bailey Sessions papers for 1674-1913 are searchable online. See www.oldbaileyonline.org
King's Bench (the highest criminal court) see TNA reference at KB2 for 1682-1985
Police Courts The quickest search is to use The Times Digital Archive and enter the name and date
Books:
David T Hawkings, *(as above)*
Ruth Paley and Simon Fowler, *Skeletons in the Cupboard* (TNA, 2009)
Stephen Wade *Tracing Your Criminal Ancestors* (Pen and Sword, 2009)

Some Latin Abbreviations in assize records
Remember that assize records are in Latin before 1733. Even after that date, these abbreviations were used:

Ca null- for *catalla nulla* no good to forfeit (a felony meant that the criminal forfeited all possessions). 'catalla' is the root of the word 'chattels'

Cog ind – for *cognovitin dictamentum* confessed to the indictment (charge)

Cul for *culpabilis* guilty

Ign for *ignoramus* 'we do not know' meaning there is no charge known.

Non cul nec re for *non culpabilis nec retraxit* not guilty, and did not flee.

Po se for *ponit se super patriam* puts himself before the country (not guilty plea)

Sus for *suspendatur* for *let him be hanged*

**

2

Cops

Police Ancestors and Where to Find Them

Consider how many thousands of people through history, particularly since the 1829 Police Act and the first Peelers, have served in one of the hundreds of police forces that have existed in British history. Your ancestor may well have been a Special Constable, as thousands of these were sworn into service in times of great emergency, such as the police strike of 1919, or even back in the 1830s at the time of the Chartist disturbances. The ancestor in question may have been a constable in a small force long ago amalgamated into a much larger police constabulary, as the process of change rationalised the structure of the police.

In the process of writing and researching my genealogy book, *Tracing Your Police Ancestors*, I discovered that this is one of the most difficult of the trades and professions to trace and understand as it developed throughout history. But there are some sources that offer useful and exciting results, and here I want to describe and explain some of them.

THE MAIN DATABASE INDEX-This is the first step in research: looking at the Index at the Open University:
www.open.ac.uk/Arts/history/policing/police-archives-guide/index.html

Sources might range from charge books to memoirs, so it is essential that some kind of general listing of holdings be consulted, and the only one in existence is now online as part of the Open University web site. This guide to archives was originally compiled by Ian Bridgeman and Martin Stallion, and then was enlarged by Clive Emsley. As the authors wrote in their preface to that extensive archive in 1989, 'The documents listed below contain a wealth of information on the ordering and control of urban and rural life from the mid-nineteenth century, on the supervision of strikes and protest marches, the treatment of aliens, the impact of twentieth century total war….'

The guide consists of an alphabetical index based on the current names of the police forces, and it includes any material not deposited at the National Archives, including items from the Metropolitan Police and the British Transport Police. The ordering is as follows:

1. Administrative items such as reports
2. Crime: crime registers, prisoners and photo albums
3. Force instructions: General orders, Memoranda etc.
4. Station Journals: occurrence Books, 'Lost and Found' and Pocket Books/Beat Books
5. Personnel: Registers, Rolls, Discipline.
6. Watch Committee and Standing Joint Committee: Minute Books / Chief Constables' Reports.
7. Miscellaneous: Special Constables etc.

Clearly, for the family historian's needs, section 5 is the most relevant. For instance, if one looks under the West Yorkshire Police

section, locating the Bradford City Police (abolished in 1974) there are many items that could relate to a family history search:
Examination of Candidates Register for 1897-1911
Register of officers and constables 1918-1945
Defaulters' Book for 1883-1896
Chief Constables' Report Books for 1902-1974
Report on insubordinate language – Sidney Chamberlain

The case of Bradford was merely a random sample to illustrate what may be found. If your ancestor was a constable, then in that particular archive for his period in office, there may only be a simple record of dates and perhaps a comment when he passed an examination. If he was insubordinate then you would have something else. In other words, as with much family history, the narrative we compile is amplified when there are events happening outside routine: anything from a major riot to an obscenity spoken while on duty. In other words, what the researcher longs for in this context is something out of the ordinary routine. Police work on the beat was very tedious of course. In the Victorian period the temptations of drink at various ports of call on the beat were too hard to resist and sackings were frequent.

HULL CITY POLICE - A CASE STUDY
The Hull City Constabulary was formed in 1836 and were absorbed into the Humberside force in 1974. The records of their staff are kept mostly at the East Riding of Yorkshire Archives, at Beverley. Their records make an excellent example of showing exactly what range and variety there are in the resources available for the family

historian locating and investigating a police ancestor. The material ranges from reports and rewards books to burial club records and superannuation or even medical records.

Superannuation records are usually one of the most substantial sources, and they provide the researcher with the opportunity to locate quite detailed information about a constable, including of course length of service, but also a career summary, and in the cases of early retirement due to ill health, even more information on the person in question. A bare list, as in this one (an extract) from the Hull Police receiving superannuation on medical grounds, provides a basis for further work:

Hull Policemen Receiving Superannuation on Medical Grounds1851-1866:
'Policeman Date pension Given Employment status' are the headings used. Then these details, for instance:
Supt. McManus May 1851 Died in post Apr. 1866
PC Cox Nov.1851 retired on medical grounds

But much more may be gleaned when the medical records and statements or requests for payments are studied. County archives will in most cases have these. Here are some examples from the East Riding Archives based on papers from the East Riding Constabulary superannuation records.

First, a general one-off payment: Aug. 17 1859 *'As required by 19 and 20 Vic. I certify that Police Sergeant William Ford burst a Blood vessel in the execution of his duty on the night of 5 June past.I*

recommend him for a gratuity of 6 months pay from the superannuation funds.'
This is a request giving career length of service:
'Superintendent Joseph Young is totally unfit for duty. Vide medical certificate C and D.
He has been a P.C. for 20 and 4/12 years, has served 10 years as a superintendent in this Riding and 14 and 9/12 have been in the present organisation.'

Note: this item has one of those extra details which add character profiles, as the surgeon has added to the medical certificate: '*I may add that he has been under me since 12 July and it was in direct opposition to my wishes that he attended the Assize at York*'

<u>At the general quarter session of the peace,
19th day of October, 1873, before the chairman and justices...</u>

*Motion: That there is a recommendation to the Chief Constable that A pension be granted to Superintendent Wilkinson who is incapable from infirmity of body to perform the duties of his office.
And that a Sergeant or Inspector be appointed to the new lock-up at St. John's Wood and also that an additional constable be appointed to the police station at Dairycotes....*
By the court,
GEO. LEEMAN
Clerk of the Peace. Then, some accounts give information regarding the areas covered by individual cases, in a specific constabulary, as in the above medical certificate.

Finally, some superannuation requests contain a more exact career summary of an officer, such as this:
'*Superintendent J D Wright has served 37 years. 3 years in Newcastle, 13 as a rural policeman and 21 years as superintendent with the present organisation.*
Similarly, George Cordukes's career was:
'*39 years as a P.C. – 10 years in the Leeds Borough Police; 6 years as a superintendent with the West Riding Constabulary and 20 years with the present organisation.*'

It may be seen from this that pension and superannuation payments, from ex gratia to proportional retirement pay, provide considerable biographical depth of material.

Step by Step Guide- Looking for John Carroll
One: start with the Open University Index at the website:
 www.open.ac.uk/Arts/history/policing/police--archives-guide/incex.html

Two :Find the area and archive in which your ancestor's constabulary exists or existed.
John Carroll was in the Hull City Police so the East Riding or Hull archives are the two repositories you need to search. The listings of material will give you the constabulary names

Three: At the archives, start with career dates and number

REWARDS BOOKS

Let's now look at the police career of John Carroll, who joined the Hull force in 1866 and was superannuated in 1896. His wife died in May, 1900 and he died a few months later.

In the Hull Police Roll we find the date of Carroll's enrolment into the police, his number, and in the first pages of what was called the Rewards Book we find a summary of his promotions, as he went from 3rd class constable in 1869 to detective sergeant in 1878. The Rewards Books also records the very common misdemeanours of officers also, such as the note on one constable who was noted as 'being drunk when on duty at 4. 20 a.m. – and this on the same record sheet as Carroll's promotion was listed, 'promoted to the rank of sergeant.' The Rewards Books also sometimes feature detailed accounts of events, as in this from 1870:

'Disobedience of orders in not going to Messrs Wilson's ship to engage a berth for a London detective inspector for Gothenborg owing to which neglect he failed to obtain information that this steamer was detained through ice impeding the navigation at Gothenborg and which information if obtained at the time the order was given might have been telegraphed to London and thus have saved the Detective Inspector an unnecessary journey from London to Hull.'

But Carroll seems never to have disgraced himself and he worked steadily through all his career.

Four: Promotions and any other events

The Rewards Book gives a summary of career details. Sometimes your ancestor was noted and named in local newspapers, and that can be a long search, but some web sites now can help with this – see the lists of web sites.

Five: the story completed
THE BURIAL CLUB

We encounter Detective Carroll next in the records of the City of Hull Police Burial Club records. Here, details of payments made for relatives and self are given, so that we learn that Ann Carroll died 21.5.1900, as written in red ink in the payment column. The same entry, in red, is made for John a little later. These professional burial clubs were an offshoot of the Friendly Society ideal; the idea was that small payments made would cover funeral costs of the officer and of close relatives, if that was desired. By 1900 when the Carrolls died, it has been calculated that over five million people in Britain subscribed to such societies. Superannuation was given for long service, and in Hull, the first superannuation was given in 1951. The officer would receive pension money and salary, and someone like Carroll would have very welcome rewards for good service.

INVESTIGATING CHARGE BOOKS

Interestingly, calendars of prisoners add a little narrative to the charge book. If a line in a calendar says, ' John Clay Oct 13. for stealing one cotton shirt, the property of Matthew Sharman' we have the next stage from the charge book, which records the constable's name, the alleged offence and the potential offender. A charge book basically records the details at the station of these basic facts, and how the prisoner was disposed of.

A typical charge book will be a huge and heavy folio volume with these headings across two pages:

Date/name/occupation/charge/ arresting officer/custody record/ magistrate/sentence and other notes. So in these records we have simply the name of the officer involved, as in this detail from 1861: *William Wass, shoemaker, was arrested by PC 47, Henry Booth, for an assault on a constable in the execution of his duty.*
And in 1862 William Wilkinson stole a heifer and was arrested by Superintendent Horsley. He was given six months in Louth gaol.

The charge books give an enlightening account of the range and nature of all levels of crime, and they also testify to the high number of assaults on police. Occasionally an officer is involved in more serious crime as in the case of Emma Taylor in 1861 who was charged with feloniously killing Ann Gray in the parish of Nickenby. She was arrested by a superintendent (no name) but was discharged at the Assizes.

A SOURCE FROM THE PROFESSIONAL PRESS

We now glance at *The Police Journal*; this publication was styled 'a quarterly review for the police forces of the empire' but in fact the material covered was very wide and a typical issue carried updates on criminal law, crime writing on notorious cases, forensic studies, explanations of the criminal legal system, research reports and of course, practical topics such as traffic lights and police boxes. Where it becomes useful to the family historian is in the correspondence, obituaries, biographical notices and listings of colonial appointments. There have been dozens of ephemeral professional magazines from the police, particularly as over the long history of the force, there have never been unions – merely the professional Police Federation. Magazines for police officers over the last century and a half have been sometimes merely leisure publications, but others have been genuinely work-related matters, and often with interesting features on the kinds of issues your ancestor faced and discussed in the tea-room.

The *Police Journal* featured lists of appointments of police officers as they went to places throughout the Empire, along with the biographical notices. In terms of correspondence, a typical example is a letter on learning Morse Code from Constable Frank Mackie of the Stirling County Constabulary, published in 1937. Many such writers among the ranks were involved in the annual King's Gold Medal Essay Competition, such as a piece on the traffic problem by R P Wilson, Chief Constable of the West Sussex Constabulary.

In 1936 there were five recipients of the award or of 'commended': as well as R P Wilson, and these were: F T Tarry of Exeter, W A Bourne Price of Bengal, Arthur Cain, a sergeant in the Metropolitan Police and R J Preston, a Salford constable.

Of all the publications that are likely to offer names and events across the country, this journal is arguably the best. If your police ancestor was a sporty type or went to work in Kenya or Palestine, he would be listed in this publication.

For the optimum use of these sources, all you need to know are the dates of service, and even if you are guessing these (and your ancestor was not in the Metropolitan Police) these will be in the superannuation records. For any force other than the London officers, the databases listed in the Open University/Police History Society listings will give you the 'lead' you need at the early stage.

The Killing of Police Sergeant Hately
Danger to law and order at the Alnwick hiring fair

Hiring and Mops

The Hiring Fair was a very old institution in English history, dating back over the centuries to the reign of Edward III, and later, in the Tudor period when affairs concerning masters and servants were regulated more forcefully, days were named on which labour could be hired, and the High Constable of the shire would define terms of pay and working conditions.

The annual fair then became a major event: we know from social history and from literature that the hiring fair, or mop fair as it was sometimes known, became an occasion when labour was hired for a year from Michaelmas to Michaelmas. Men and women would stand in line, set to show off their trades and skills, so that L W Cowie described, 'cowman had a tuft of cowhair, carters a piece of whipcord, shepherds a tuft of sheepswool and thatchers a fragment of women straw, while servant-girls carried a mop or wore a white apron.'

The token was taken when the individual was given work, but of course that description suggests a smooth, organised system. In fact, the fairs were occasions at which drink might flow too freely, competition might become too heated, and old jealousies and resentments might explode. No doubt the hired men and women, when the fast-penny was pressed into their hand to seal the bargain, felt in need of something to wet their whistle. All around them were the amusements of the fair, and fun was in the air. Pleasure could easily transmute into aggression.

Death at Alnwick

At Alnwick in Northumberland at the March Fair in 1875, the jollification changed into a riot, and in the midst of the violence and unrest was the constable. As one account has it: '... the said [Sergeant] John Hately came to his death whilst in the execution of his duty in endeavouring to quiet a disturbance which took place... on the hiring day of the 6th of March.' He left a widow and eight children.

For the previous twenty years, legislation had slowly been professionalising the provincial police, and progress was uneven. But what was given least consideration was the safety of an officer. Hately was hit by a stone, flung at him from the crowd, and he died of the injuries sustained. Here was a brave man, standing out and being counted, as it were, in the force for order and reason. He paid for that bravery with his life. What had the law done to organise and streamline the force around him?

The most significant legislation came in 1856 with the County and Borough Police Act. After the report of a Select Committee on Police in 1853, it was made compulsory for county forces to be created and for some amalgamations to be effected. To supervise this, special offices were created to be called Her Majesty's Inspectors of Constabulary. The report of 1853 had stressed the vagrancy problem, as that was considered to be a major cause of crime, and in the larger rural counties we can see the implementations of his

Act taking that into consideration. In Lincolnshire, for example, the reports on the Lincolnshire Constabulary by the Chief Constable in 1857 given to the Joint Police Committee lists the strength of the force: Lindsey had seven superintendents and 43 constables; Kesteven had one superintendent and 20 constables, and Holland had one superintendent and 16 constables. The magistrates met in 1856 'convened by the Lord Lieutenant and held in the castle of Lincoln in October, 1856 for the proper taking into consideration the Act 19 and 20 Vic. Cap. 69 to render more effectual the police in county boroughs of England and Wales.'

As to the important features such as ratio of police officers to population in the counties, these varied greatly. In Norfolk, for instance, there were 196 officers in 1856, a ratio to population of 1/3451. In Dorset there were only twelve men at the time. Essentially, the police officer at the time of Hately's death, had no hope of assistance in times of trouble: later in the century, there were death and burial clubs of most constabularies, and superannuation came in. Some forces, such as Hull for instance, had superannuation funds as early as the 1860s, but for many, if the worst happened, it was a case of charity and humane responses to personal tragedy. Hately's force did have a superannuation fund, but with eight children that was hardly adequate. Still, as a deed of 2nd May 1875 states, £81 was given 'as a gratuity' from the police superannuation fund 'after providing for the immediate wants of the widow and family.'

A Hard Time for Peelers

By the later Victorian years, the public were becoming so well informed and opinionated about the 'Peelers' that letters to the newspapers were common, and opinions strong, as in this letter to the *Manchester Guardian* in 1873 in response to a debate on the tendency of constables to arrest anyone supine on the streets: 'We have no wish to be hard upon the constable. Speaking generally, he is not, and cannot be expected to be, a man of discriminating mind, and he usually has a good deal of work on hand – work which, without any fault of character in himself, must tend to develop a cynical faculty. Even a policeman, however, ought to know that men and women may fall powerless to the ground from other causes than excessive drinking.' The attitude is typical of what was developing: an ambivalent attitude, sympathy mixed with negative representations.

In other words, the individual officer was a vulnerable figure. Hately tried to stop a riot. The result was that the reputation of the hiring fair for trouble and disorder was confirmed, and the community was left with a widow and eight orphans to somehow help and supervise. Documentation shows that there was, in fact, the most stunning and impressive response to the sergeant's violent death. Notices were posted across a number of parishes. The aim was to 'raise a fund for their immediate and future benefit.' Subscriptions were called for at banks and stationers' shops. The response was massive and overwhelming.

By June 21st 1875, when the trustees of the Hately Fund arranged to meet, a sum of £743-1s-4p had been raised. A list of subscribers between May 15 and May 27 that year has no less than 39 people, and they had given sums as small as one guinea, up to large amounts such as £5 from C.W Orde. By June a huge list was issued, properly in print, listing several hundred donations of sums between

2s 6d down to one shilling. His Grace the Duke of Northumberland, at Alnwick Castle, gave £25.

The Community rallies Around Mary

The records of the work undertaken on behalf of Mrs Mary Hately by the trustees shows what could be achieved, in those dangerous days before proper social welfare and support, by sheer energy and commitment, done in recognition of a deed of courage. In fact, what the trustees did was what every right-thinking person of wealth did at the time: invest in railways and in the government. Everyone was doing it, from the Rothschilds downwards. A letter from the trustees describes the matter:

'It is also declared that the said trustees shall have full power to invest the Trust funds in government or real securities or in Railway Stock, where the whole capital has been called up... and that all indemnity clauses under The statute (22nd and 23 Victoria Chapter 35) to save trustees from risk, shall

Be considered as incorporated... into this deed.'

It was decided that the Trust should last '19 and a half years at least' and in the formal agreement concerning the fund's investment, there was a remarkable degree of attention given to Mary's welfare, separate from a long list of trust sums held for all the children. The deed says that all sums not apportioned for the children are 'for the benefit of the said Mary Hately for her life for her sole and separate use only and not to be subject to the debts or control of any husband she might have...'

Mary Hately was forty years old when her husband died. She must have been astonished at the local response to the sad death of her husband of course: the result of that flying chunk of rock at the hiring fair highlights two important and fascinating mid-Victorian elements of social history: the fragile nature of every community in tough times, when hard farming work ground down the working population to seek consolation in drink and in high-jinks, and naturally, the dangerous nature of those guardians of law who faced the trouble head-on. There was solidarity when tragedy followed, and Mary Hately would have noticed that, aside from the huge sums given to her by tradesmen and professional people in her community, there was a very large sum of over £27 raised by the men at the Northumberland Constabulary, and what stands out, apart from the £7 paid by his superintendent, is the £7 12s.5p from a simple constable – P.C. Spence. We have to speculate that this man was a close friend indeed, maybe the man who grew up with him in the force.

Where to Find Police Documents
The documents are found mainly in the county record offices. Archives will generally have a full listing of holdings in the index books. The key word is *Constabulary* or *police* of course. In addition to the Open University listings of archive sources, these are useful places to check out:

Police Museums and History Societies. England:
The Hampshire Constabulary History Society
Southern Support and Training Headquarters

Victoria House,
Netley
Hampshire

Ripon Prison and Police Museum,
St. Marygate,
Ripon,
North Yorks

Surrey Police Museum,
Mount Browne,
Sandy lane,
Guildford,
Surrey GU3 1 HG

British Transport Police History Society,
15-17 Tavistock Place,
London WC1 9SY

The Police History Society,
64, Nore Marsh Road,
Wootton Bassett,
Wiltshire SN4 8BH

Republic of Ireland
Garda Siochana Museum and Archives,
The Records Tower,
Dublin Castle, Dublin 2

Scotland

The Glasgow Police Museum,
68, St Andrews Square,
Glasgow G1 5PR

Web sites for Police History
www.policehistory.com
This is a site for police history in Ireland.
www.policememorial.org.uk
This lists all officers in the United Kingdom who lost their lives on duty.
www.blacksheepindex.co.ukPOLNOTES.htm
This is a fascinating resource for tracing police ancestors through newspaper reports.
www.btp.police.uk This is the British Transport Police site.

**

3

Villains

Today there are an increasing number of resources to help you do the detective work involved in this. We now have the Criminal registers from Ancestry.co.uk. These cover the years 1791 -1892 and they offer materials relating to all categories of trial. That means that for most researchers there will be sources available from quarter sessions and assizes. The new facility allows you to start with a search relating to name and date/place of birth, then this leads to court records to access and study.

There are many more criminal records, and these comprise documents relating to each stage of a convict's trajectory through the system. Most of these are court and prison records, and today The National Archives and County Record Offices have the bulk of them. In these archives are found assize records, prison registers and calendars of prisoners: the fundamental material on which you can base all further research into the ancestor's life.

Until 1971 when the assizes were replaced by crown courts, the criminal law procedure had been in these phases:

1.The initial hearing would be at a coroner's court (if there was a suspicious death) or at a magistrate's court. There would be quarter sessions

2. After the first hearing, if the crime was a felony, it went to the assizes. **Summary and indictable:** A summary offence may be tried by a magistrate only, whereas an indictable offence has to be tried before a jury. This relates also to the definitions of *felony and misdemeanour*: a felony, until the Criminal Law Act of 1967 was a serious offence, and before 1870, it meant that the convict would forfeit all lands and chattels, and often being sentenced to death as well. A misdemeanour was a less extreme offence, usually tried summarily. In the records and texts relating to your ancestor, these words will occur.

These were held from the 13th century until 1971. The system had its origins in which two judges would hold the sovereign's court twice a year. These tried criminal cases and civil. From 1550, records provide details of such offences as homicide, infanticide and major theft. Before 1733 assize records are in Latin and the main records are indictments (statements of charges); depositions (written evidences) and gaol books or minutes (lists of accused persons and summaries of cases heard). If there are no assize records surviving, then there are sheriffs' assize vouchers, located at THA E389 and also, for writs, the King's Bench records. The King's Bench.

The Gentleman's Magazine published details of the assize circuits, such as this entry from the 1819 issue: 'Spring Circuits, 1819: Norfolk, Lord Chief Justice Abbott and baron Graham: Aylesbury, March 4, Bedford March 10, Huntingdon March 13, Thetford March 20, Bury St Edmund's March 26.'

3. From the assizes, if convicted, the accused would either have a prison sentence, be sent to an asylum, or (until the 1860) be transported to the colonies.

Step by Step Guide

This is the process for researching a criminal life, including the criminal career of Charles Peace as the example, incorporating the Ancestry.co.uk facility where possible.

1. Find The Criminal Register

These records are mostly held at TNA, but there will be others scattered around the CRO's. If you know that your ancestor was convicted then, if the register has survived, the papers will be at Kew. The criminal register gives physical details of the person, place of birth and place of abode, next of kin, trade and level of literacy. Peace was in Armley Gaol, Leeds before his death in 1879.

2. Find the Calendar of Prisoners

A list of accused persons was made before a court case began. By the close of the eighteenth century these lists, calendars of prisoners, were issued in print, so they may be found in TNA or in local CRO's. Before that time they were in court papers often referred to as Order Books and Process Books. These sheets give much the same information as the registers, but they have more details of the offence, and details of the person who committed them.

There are photos also in the Ancestry database, available online with a subscription. There are even pictures of celebrity criminals such as Charles Peace, but there are photos of every person who went to prison – from the 1860s onwards – and these are in all prison records where available, and may also be found in police records where petty thieves were photographed and pictures attached to the police materials. These are often available at the CRO's.

3. Look at the Court Records

For this case study, the Ancestry Criminal registers provides the sources. Using the facility, you enter the name, date of birth and place of birth of the criminal, and then lists of sources are given. These only include trial records within the main system. If your ancestor appeared in a church or other court, they will not be here.

The amount of material available here will vary according to the seriousness of the offence. For most petty criminals, the record will be short and precise, but the CRO will have quarter sessions records and these will include a statement of the accusation in the form of a recognizance. This describes the offence, stated by a citizen, formalising matters in the form of a bond for the accuser to appear in court. At quarter sessions, there is usually a fairly detailed account of proceedings.

In the case of Charles Peace, after committing a murder in Manchester for which he let another man take the sentence, he moved to London after a second murder in Sheffield, and lived under an assumed name: John Ward. In this record from the Ancestry Criminal registers facility, he appears with that name and is sentenced to life. This was at the Old Bailey, and so was reported in full in the Old Bailey Sessions papers, available to read online.

Newspapers, from around the late eighteenth century (*The Times* appeared in 1785) began to give very full reports of crimes, and also *The Annual Register* covered assizes and some quarter sessions, published at the end of each year. Charles Peace, after his arrest in

London, was then linked to the Sheffield murder and sent to Leeds for trial. This record, from Ancestry, we have Peace listed in the sentences from the West Yorkshire Assizes and he is there sentenced to death.

4. Newspapers

You will find a newspaper report on the Peace trial from The Times Digital Archive. But if you are not sure of the dates or place of the trial for your ancestor, then use The Black Sheep Index, which lists (online) names and dates of newspaper references. If your ancestor committed a robbery somewhere in Britain and you know the dates of the person's life, if they were mentioned in a newspaper they will be listed in this index. For Charles Peace, there are dozens of entries, of course.

5. Check other Prison Records

After sentencing from assizes, other courts held by other bodies, or from the Old Bailey, the convict, from early Stuart years through to the 1860s, be transported, first to America and later, after 1780, to Australia. Convict records are substantial, but in terms of prisons, the criminal may have been in a prison hulk before transportation, and these records are at TNA. If there was a prison sentence within the Prison estate in Britain, then there will almost certainly be other records, above the bare listings in registers and calendars. Prison doctors and governors kept journals for instance, so these will in some cases have been preserved. These may even have letters and statements by the prisoner, preserved in the papers, in this note from Charles Peace while in Armley gaol.

After all these searches, you will have a fairly substantial account of the criminal's life after sentencing. The categories of documents all come within either court or prison records, unless there was transportation or there was a case of insanity. For the latter, asylum records are in many instances very thorough, and again, are often in CRO's. There are registers of admission for these and at TNA there are returns from workhouses and asylums for the years 1834 to 1909.

An Appeal for Clemency
There is also the further stage in research: your ancestor may have appealed against the sentence. There was no court of criminal appeal until 1907, but there were letters petitioning pardon, to the Home Secretary after the Home Office was established in 1782, and always, since Medieval times, to the sovereign. The story of Elizabeth Ward is an example.

Elizabeth Ward was only seventeen when she very nearly killed her sister-in-law. She was destined to hang for it, in spite of a plea to the judge, which was of no use, as he would not commute the sentence, despite her youth. He thought she should be an exemplar case to deter others. *The Times* reported it, picking out this aspect: ' One enormous case occurred at York – that of Elizabeth Ward, seventeen years of age, who was convicted of the horrid crime of administering poison to her sister, and is to suffer death.' The paper got the facts slightly wrong, but it picked out the repugnance of the affair.

In July 1816 Elizabeth went from her home in Rothwell into Leeds (only a few miles away) and bought two ounces of arsenic. She was seen the next day mixing white powder into porridge, and she was seen by her little brother George, whose statements later would be very important. Her sister-in-law Charlotte was the intended victim, and the fact that she noticed something amiss with the food is quite astonishing through modern eyes. Most poison victims were unlikely to do this, of course, as the natural inclination is to eat or drink with ease and with speed. But Charlotte for some reason sensed something wrong and she noticed the white substance in the jug, locking this in a cupboard. Even more impressive was her forcing herself to be sick to vomit up what tiny traces had gone into her blood. As for Elizabeth, she was seen by little George throwing the rest of the food away.

Sensible Charlotte then went for medical advice and consulted a druggist, Mark Poskitt. He and another chemist tested vomit and found arsenic traces. The teenager had failed in her quest to kill, but it had been a close-run thing. In most cases, the victim would have swallowed enough to kill or at least to create long hours of horrible suffering. Elizabeth was charged, naturally. There was a motive, and the girl explained this herself when questioned, saying that after Elizabeth's mother had died a few months before these events, Charlotte had become the centre of power in the home and young Elizabeth did not like that at all. But Charlotte came through the effects of the small amount of poison she had taken and went to the magistrate to give the facts.

Nine-year-old George had to testify against his big sister, and he had plenty to say. This was at York Assizes, just a week after the attempted murder. It is stunning to report that there was no defence lawyer for the girl, and yet five witnesses were called. The teenager was allowed to question these people but as we can imagine, she could not put much of a coherent argument together and could simply protest her innocence. There were three druggists lined up against her, and the one from whom she had bought the arsenic in Leeds recognised her: she was doomed.

She was sentenced to death, and only then did another story come through. There may well have been a case of insanity in this, but the judge found no reason to commute the sentence.

Even that process was long and uncertain. The sovereign George III was mentally incapacitated and the appeal went to the Home Secretary Lord Sidmouth and then to the Regent. There was support for the girl in high places, though, and here there was a Yorkshire lobby, from no less a dignitary than Lord Lascelles. He it was who brought about a postponement of the hanging at first, and then with more time, the city of York and other groups across the county put together a petition that went to the Prince Regent, who directed a reprieve.

Useful Addresses and Sources
Courts:
Assizes: Early assize records are at The National Archives (TNA) at JUST 1-4.
For later assizes: see the TNA guide on assize records under 'research guides' on the web site.
Old Bailey Sessions papers have these major records covering 1674-1913
King's Bench: TNA has these papers: known as the Upper Bench 1649-1660 at KB 10

Quarter Sessions records are at the County record Offices.

Prisons:
See TNA guide at www.nationalarchives.go.uk/catalogue/Rdleaflet.
For a quick reference to all TNA sources, see Amanda Bevan, Tracing Your Ancestors in the National Archives (National Archives, 2009)
Also all prison records are listed and explained in David T Hawkings' *Criminal Ancestors* (History Press, 2010)
Black Sheep Index – for a first newspaper search– www.blacksheepindex.com

Trouble Shooting
• What if your ancestor is not recorded in the mainstream criminal justice sources? Try the church (ecclesiastical) courts. These cases would often be reported in the newspapers, and may also be found in regional or diocesan church records for your area.
• The person may have been in the forces: then military and admiralty courts may be the place to look. Again, as well as TNA, The Times gave very thorough reports on these, and the digital archive covers 1785-1985.
The case may have been heard in a civil court. Although civil business was different from criminal actions, the civil courts often dealt with matters which today would be crimes (what we now call 'corporate manslaughter' for instance).

Sent to Van Dieman's Land
The use of transportation by the British government for dealing with criminals stretches back to 1607, and the notion of establishing this

punishment within the criminal justice system begins officially with the Transportation Act of 1718. This started the use of America as the main location of convict settlement, but after the War of Independence and the loss of the American colonies, Britain looked elsewhere for distant colonies, and in 1787 the first fleet sailed from Portsmouth for Botany Bay.

The settlement of the mainland of Australia had begun, but in 1803 a young lieutenant called John Bowen was sent to create a British foothold in the south of Tasmania. A year later, Hobart was established, and Van Dieman's Land was named. Abel Tasman had been to Tasmania in 1642 and he named it Anthoonij van Diemanslandt after the Governor-General of the Dutch East Indies.

The name was to resonate through popular culture and the press through to our own day, with oral history, folk music and film maintaining the image of the place as one of the worst, most brutal penal colonies in history. There is some exaggeration in that, as many of the most horrendous destinations for convicts were in the secondary prison locations around Australia, but Van Dieman's Land is a name that has dominated the criminal history of the antipodes.

In the Regency years, when there were over 200 capital crimes on the statute books, transportation was seen as a viable and desirable alternative to long prison sentences, but unfortunately, the hulks (prison ships in estuaries) were used as gaols before the prisoners were transported, and it is estimated that between 1776 and 1795 over a third of the 5,722 prisoners died. One writer of the time wrote: 'There were confined in these floating dungeons nearly 600 men, most of them double ironed... with horrible effects rising from rattling chains and the filth and vermin naturally produced by such a crowd of miserable inhabitants.'

The Convicts

Who were these people-75,000 in total–sent to Van Dieman's Land? They certainly had a reputation, becoming known as 'Vandemonians' so that the play on words would suggest something devilish and evil. The fact is that many were criminals who robbed or assaulted through desperation and suffering; poachers and pickpockets, sellers of stolen goods, and of course nasty characters who would have hanged for serious crimes were also destined for one of the Tasmanian colonies. Typical examples are these cases from 1833:

William Stephenson (21) charged with stealing a black cart mare *transported for life*

James Bedford (41) shoe maker, charged with feloniously killing a yearling sheep *transported for life*

Isaac Johnson (46) charged with feloniously stealing one pair of boots *14 years trans.*

But there were also political prisoners, such as the Welsh Chartists who conducted a rising in Newport in 1839; they were convicted of treason and the sentences commuted to life at Port Arthur for their radical beliefs, such as the right to vote and the abolition of child labour. There was also William Smith O'Brien, who led an insurrection at Ballingarry, Tipperary and who was condemned to death but then he was sent to Port Arthur and was there from 1848 to his release in 1854. As his status was political, he had a separate house, prominent on the slope above the penitentiary.

There were some transportees who were famous of course. George Loveless, one of the Tolpuddle Martyrs of 1834, was sent to Port Arthur (the others were sent to Sydney). The 'Martyrs' had been involved in attempting to form a trade union, and so Loveless was a special case for the authorities in Hobart. He was constantly under supervision, as his biographer wrote, 'Loveless reported three interrogations –one on board ship and two ashore – of which two were conducted by the police magistrate and one by the Governor himself...'

Among the Hobart Town convicts there were 'hard cases' – known as incorrigibles – and when the assignment system started, in which convicts were assigned to settlers to work, there was friction, resentment and all kinds of problems related to work and integration.

The Prison Settlements and the Establishment of Port Arthur

Before the penitentiary at Port Arthur, there were convict bases at Macquarie and Maria Island; Macquarie was established in 1821 mainly to take Huon pine trees for boat-building, but by 1830 there were severe problems, the main one being that the harbour there was very dangerous. Maria Island also did not really work, and escapes were common. A surveyors' report then described the suitability of a bay within an isthmus. Thomas Scott wrote that the place was ' a deep and safe harbour, with stands of timber on all sides coming down to the water's edge.' The first period of the convict settlement there was one in which security and a tough regime were a priority. The geography was the main factor: the Tasman Peninsula is joined to Forestier's Peninsula by a narrow strip of land known as Eaglehawk Neck, and so that was the only possible escape route by land for escapees. Otherwise they would have had to cope with the ocean or with the vast Norfolk Bay.

On Eaglehawk Neck a line of huge, vicious dogs was in place. There were also dogs and armed troops on the shore across from the isthmus so that any convict who tried to swim, and who survived the sharks, came ashore in front of the mastiffs. One report described the arrangement: 'The land is only seventy-eight yards across, and double sentinels are posted day and night… a line of eighteen dogs extends across… and being kept separate, are most ferocious…'

The Regime
Wearing his Hessian jacket and trousers, the convict would rise with the bell at dawn, have a drink of hot water and flour called *skilly*, and start the day's hard labour. He would have Sunday free and on Saturday afternoons he could have a bath and some recreation. As today, there were areas for exercise and of course the chapel for worship. This was built on the principle of the 'silent system' so that each convict sat in a cubicle from which he could see no others, and so his silent prayer was aided by isolation.

Discipline, particularly under George Arthur, was hard. Flogging was used, as it was in the army and at times in British gaols at home for the most recalcitrant offenders. The man being punished would be fastened to a three-legged frame, then placed in a bath of salt after the cat o' nine tails had been applied. There was always a doctor present in case things went too far and life was threatened.

There was a system in place that used convicts as constables, and as with prisons through history, there was 'prisoner power' in which punishments were applied for unacceptable behaviour. Men who had 'grassed' and who were sent to another settlement or to court for witness duty, had to return, and there they would face retribution. There were cases in which such men begged the Governor to be sent elsewhere, to escape death at the hands of fellow prisoners.

Public Works and Local Gaols
Convicts worked in gangs on building projects, and a typical example of this is the work done at Richmond, north of Hobart, which was named in 1824 and developed quickly; it became a military centre and needed convict labour, and a gaol to hold them. This form of slave labour (which in effect is what it was) enabled roads and bridges to be made. The bridge at Richmond was built by convicts in 1825, originally called Bigge's bridge, and it is the oldest bridge still in use in the whole of Australia. Further up the coast towards Bicheno, travellers may see a classic example of this work done by labour gangs, at Spiky Bridge, completed in1843.

The gaol at Richmond is typical of the type of small local establishment needed to house the convicts. It is a grim place, with solitary confinement cells and a flogging yard. It must have been hell for the prisoners: in the 1830's the gaoler complained that he had an overcrowding problem, with 40 prisoners held in a space of only nineteen square metres. The gaol had twelve sleeping rooms, a small airing yard and eleven day-rooms. There were separate solitary cells for women and a cookhouse. The remains of the foundation used for the flogging frame are still visible, and it must have been a harrowing experience to suffer punishment there.

When not out on local building projects, convicts in the gaol would fill their time by painting, cleaning, doing all the housework chores, and sometimes having a little recreation such as draughts, as we know from a draught board which was cut into a floor.

The Assignment System
Convicts mostly started their penal time as assigned labour. Some of this was on public works, but also many prisoners were assigned to settlers. Governor Arthur was strict in his rules concerning this system, insisting on firm discipline and religious worship and bible study within the working week. Alcohol was strictly forbidden, and in fact the masters taking on convicts were directed to force their convict-workers to pray and to observe the Sabbath; they even had to buy bibles for the convicts.

As Robert Hughes makes clear in his massive account of transportation, *The Fatal Shore*, without assignment there would have been no colony in Van Dieman's Land. He points out that there was no labour but convict labour and that ' The mere fact of living as a free settler in a penal colony meant that a man must accept the paramount values of penal discipline.'

There were all kinds of difficulties in the system of course. Peter Brannon, for instance, who was just twelve when sentenced to life transportation for stealing a sock, was assigned to a Mrs Green in Launceston, where he was constantly rebellious and disobedient. He was always answering charges and appearing at trials; his punishment was to be put on public works, but he absconded and was then given a period of hard labour. Patrick Murphy, from Liverpool, ran off from his assignment with Thomas Reibey at Entally House, Launceston, and his punishment was work in a chain gang, constantly in irons.

Worship and Burial

For many of the convicts, their destination was an unmarked grave on the Isle of the Dead, out in the bay beyond the penitentiary; it was used from 1833, and a minister of the time described it in his journal: 'This it appeared to me, would be a secure, undisturbed resting place where the departed prisoners might lie together until the morning of the resurrection. No stone marks where he slumbers, as no tombstones or other mark is allowed to be placed at the head of the graves.'

The religious life was crucially important of course, as the concept of the prison in the Victorian period was that it should include an effort towards salvation and redemption, and a long period for reflection on past ill deeds done to others. The separate prison chapel was conceived along the lines of the first chapels in the new convict prisons back home in London, such as Pentonville. Henry Mayhew's description of the typical chapel is exactly what Port Arthur's place of worship would have been like:

'The seats are divided off in the same manner as the pit-stalls at a theatre, but in appearance they resemble a small box or pew...the reader has to imagine the ordinary pews of a church to be arranged

on an inclined plane, one above the other.. and each divided into a series of compartments just large enough to hold one person...'

The Sunday routine included opportunity for that introspection which the Victorians believed to be an essential part of the work towards reform. When the new penitentiaries were built, the chapel and time with chaplains was considered to be integral to the prison establishment.

Care and Medical Provision

Clearly, with hard physical work at the heart of the penal regime, and the frequency of infectious disease in the prison community, the medical men were of paramount importance. In fact, for the journey from Britain over the oceans to Van Dieman's Land, the surgeons' logs and journals provide some of the best information for researchers on the convicts and the illnesses they suffered.

At Port Arthur, one considerable achievement in terms of health and care was the building of an asylum and a hospital. The latter was opened for business in 1842, made of brick and sandstone; though there had originally been a small wooden hospital. The place had four wards, with facilities for around 80 patients. As with military provision in these matters, the system included convict orderlies. Although there were limitations in medical provision, one interesting point is that the food available was recorded as being of good quality. Reports often noted that the convicts' food was better than that provided back home in Britain.

The asylum was not made until the end of transportation, but it illustrates an important development: the convicts who had stayed in Tasmania and who were free after their ticket of leave (a kind of release on licence) and eventual freedom. The fact that there were many people with mental illness problems indicates some of the emotional and mental turmoil and suffering of those who had been in fact banished from their families and from their homeland. The various shades of depressive illness we now recognise were at that time only understood in very limited ways. But again, this reflected the same developments back home, as new large-scale local asylums were built from the mid-century.

The End of Transportation
The last two ships to arrive in Van Dieman's Land came in 1851. There had been a steady increase in numbers sent there as fewer were sent to New South Wales, and just before the final ships. There had been around 5,000 arriving each year. All transportation to the place was abolished in 1853 and two years later the island was renamed Tasmania. Finally, in 1868 all transportation to Australia generally ceased. The number of convicts who had made the journey there over the previous eighty years was approximately 162,000.

An 'old colonist' writing to *The Times* in 1853 took issue with some statistics, and his comments give an insight into the state of affairs at the time the ships stopped arriving in Hobart: 'The noble earl says that of the convicts sent out, 99 out of a hundred were so far reformed that after their liberation they maintained themselves by honest industry instead of crime... If the proportion of criminals permanently reformed had been given as 1 out of 100, it would have been much nearer the truth.'

But on the credit side, the case of Abraham Hood shows that people changed; he had been sentenced to transportation for stealing a horse, but by 1829 he was working as a constable in Hobart, then he became a watchman at Port Arthur, and finally entered settlement life as a baker, which is what his trade had been at home in Dalkeith.

A Convict Family

We know a lot about Snowden Dunhill, a Yorkshireman convicted of theft from a granary in 1813, because he wrote his autobiography. He became an overseer at Port Arthur but could keep on the right side of the law, and he was found trying to sell a razor and also he was caught smoking in his quarters. Snowden was to die there, and he is buried on the Isle of the Dead. When he first arrived in Australia, he wrote 'Arrived at Botany Bay, I was soon disposed of, and commenced in good earnest the life of a slave. Hard-worked, half-starved, ill-fed and worse clothed, such is the fate of the hapless convict.'

His wife, Sarah, was convicted of stealing two geese and was given a seven-year sentence. After spending time in Sydney, she managed to be transferred to Port Arthur to be with Snowden, and she found religion while in Hobart, even starting some teaching work. At her trial she was called 'an atrocious criminal' and all her children but one experienced transportation. Snowden and Sarah's son, George, was hanged for stealing lambs.

The Dunhills, particularly Snowden, won a certain amount of fame in Victorian literature; the great writer and historian, Sabine Baring-Gould, wrote a long account of Snowden in his book

Yorkshire Oddities (1874) in which he wrote that ' Snowden gradually sank into habitual drunkenness and was suspected of reverting to his old tricks of petty larceny.'

Further Information
Useful Books
The Convict Ships 1787-1868(Brown and Ferguson, 1985)
Bound for Australia, David T Hawkings (Phillimore, 2010)
Criminal Ancestors, David T. Hawkings (History Press, 2010)
The Fatal Shore, Robert Hughes (Vintage, 2003)

Web Sites
TNA Transportation to Australia 1787-1868 (there is a valuable research guide on site)
www.portarthur.org.au
www.records.nsw.gov.au
www.rootsweb.ancestry.com
www.tasfhs.org This site enables detailed searches, and includes access to a range of documents from Tasmania with a wealth of information on convicts and their records.

**

Young Offenders at Point Puer
As the records of the Old Bailey show, there was a large number of convictions of children in this period. Boys convicted of minor crimes (in modern terms) were based in Hobart until 1834 when many were sent to Port Arthur. The boys had created problems in

prison and on assignment and a solution was needed to a growing social furore about them. The answer was a site at Point Puer, (*Puer* being Latin for 'boy') around the bay from Port Arthur. This included a school and dormitories and gradually this became the central destination for juvenile offenders, and between 1838 and 1841 over a thousand boys were sent there.

The regime there was hard – a boot camp and reformatory combined – with the boys out of bed and ready for work by five in the morning, followed by inspections and several hours of work. The military basis of the regime included division into 'messes' and the use of 'corporals' in each mess.

A typical juvenile there was William Bickle, sentenced to seven years at Devon Assizes for stealing a watch, at just eleven years old he was destined for Point Puer. But he was not reformed: he had 65 charges against him while resident there, and spent 172 days in solitary confinement. Even after release in 1841, when assigned to a civilian, he was rebellious and did a year's hard labour back at Port Arthur. He was eventually released in 1843.

Bars to Progress: Finding Past Prisoners

A query from a reader to a genealogy magazine regarding an ancestor who was recorded as being in Pentonville prison in 1911 led to a strenuous effort to navigate the records of a previous criminal justice system. That research will always demand a knowledge of the particular legislation and penal provision at the time in question, and the challenge is sometimes impossible to overcome. The proverbial brick wall arrived when further research tried in vain to find out why the man, Thomas Challis, was serving time inside. Several avenues of enquiry were attempted, including a determined trawl of sources by researcher, Amber Strang, covering calendars of indictments, calendars of prisoners and minutes of evidence. No Thomas (or Abraham – his other name)- was located.

In a search for a prisoner in the family story, this situation leaves only one option: newspaper reports. The Old Bailey sessions papers brought nothing, and the digital archives also had no Challis in law and court reports who might have offered the family history detective a lead into more of a 'paper chase' elsewhere. The reader's only recourse now is to search local newspapers.

The reason for this is that prison records are rarely complete, and Pentonville records have eluded myself and other researchers in the past on other occasions. But apart from lost records, there is another element to prison records preservation that researcher should know about. This concerns a Prison Service Order first issued in 1995 and again in 1999. Under the Public Records Acts of 1958 and 1967, records 'of historical and public interest' should be selected before they have existed for thirty years and transferred from prisons to local archive collections.

Over the years, there has been a complicated basis regarding prison records kept on site in the offices of the prison administration. Recently, I have written histories of two local prisons. In one of them, I saw a batch of prisoner records from the 1950's in a cabinet and I was told that these were going to be burned. In another prison, an officer told me that records had been given to a local organisation and that when an exhibition in the prison was planned, the organisation would not return the records. The reason for an odd situation which means that some prison records are at the CRO and others are still in the prison is that the Prison Service order has this directive:

'Destruction of Old Records :There is no need to keep records more than 30 years old which are of no historical interest and which are not in administrative use. Your archivist will indicate which records are of value, and you can destroy the rest.'

Historians will cringe with apprehension at the statement. What if some Governors allowed only a portion of records to be checked by archivists? It may be the case that in some localities, the administration see prisoner records as sensitive and do not want to take any risk of offence to relatives and victims by having any chance of certain records seeing print.

Also, amateur historians, sheer enthusiasts for the past, may have been given the role of choosing and selecting materials. The result has been that there are gaps in the records, and hence the reader's problem.

The rules are clear regarding the period of time that must elapse before a member of the public can see prison records:

Execution records and registers of officers: *40 years after last use*
Governors' journals, chaplains' journals, medical officers' journals, visiting committee rota and minute books and condemned cell occurrence books: *70 years after last use*
Prisoners' calendars with identification of victims:*100 years after last use*

The Prison Service Order specified that the records kept in the prison included more recent records (under 30 years) and plans of the site or anything relating to security of course. It is not difficult to find reasons for these rulings. In HMP Lincoln for instance, there were Sinn Fein prisoners in the Edwardian period, including Eamon de Valera, and the doctor's journal contains information on the treatment of those men. But the political repercussions of that source material being open in earlier times are not hard to imagine.

There is one course of action regarding more recent records: a letter to the Home Office. If knowledge of prisoners in more recent years is needed, the directions are given clearly on the web site of the Prison Service HQ Library (based at Abell House, London): 'Not all records are kept, especially those of short sentence prisoners. You need to write a letter giving the full name of the inmate and the year they were in prison and if possible the name of the prison and the court of first conviction, and quoting the Data Protection Act.' There is a charge for this as well, currently £10. Of course, this is full of difficulties, partly because the identity and status of the letter-writer need to be verified.

Basically, what has happened over the years is that in the early twentieth century many records were lost. After that there were many *ad hoc* decisions made about records and factors concerning storage space were obviously a consideration. Before the 1958 Act there was very likely a notable variation in practice across the Prison Service. The Prison Service Order was a sensible attempt to streamline record preservation and current practice, and Governors definitely needed this advice. However, the needs of family historians were hardly a priority at the time.

On the positive side, local record offices are very helpful in making clear the records available and the guidelines for access. At the Lincolnshire Archives web site, for instance, there is a clear listing of material, and this note: 'Lincoln Prison opened on its current site in 1872. At first it housed men and women, but at some point between 1905 and 1913 women ceased to be admitted, being sent instead to Nottingham. There are unfortunately few surviving records for the years 1872-1911. .... There are also a few later gaps in the main series of Admission Registers and journals; it is hoped that the missing items may be discovered one day.' That is very helpful, and it also explains what is probably the case in most counties.

Researchers into criminal history will often encounter those words: ' There are a few later gaps' but persistence is essential, and the human web of social activity and relationships will offer other areas of enquiry. Fortunately for researchers, most convicts in the past have re-offended and their names will appear elsewhere. I once investigated an offender whose crime was committed in Manchester and found his name eventually in Dartmoor.

When these gaps occur, the newspaper reports are the only plan B in most cases. We then have to rely on sheer persistence and the serendipity factor, because there are no indexes of local paper content except for recent years in most libraries. One facility that may be helpful for anyone researching a prisoner is the Black Sheep Index. For a small fee, this makes available newspaper items involving the criminal ancestor, and it is possible to check a massive alphabetical index online with dates and the reason for the appearance of the person in the press.

This is at www.blacksheepindex.co.uk

As a coda to this topic, returning to the search for Thomas/Abraham Challis, it is not uncommon for prisoners to become 'invisible' for various reasons. They may never do anything that would put their name on a prison record sheet ('keeping the nose clean') and they may change their name on release. But there is one other course of action in this case. In 1907 the first probation service was established, and before that there were the London police court missionaries. The reader, and anyone else reading this with a similar problem, may try probation records. After all, most prisoners (even today) leaving prison and stepping back into society, need that kind of help and support.

**

4

Trials

If your ancestor was a 'black sheep' who fell foul of the law, or if he or she merely offended the local church in some small way, they could have been destined for a court appearance. For researching family history it is essential to have a grasp of which courts were important and where their records are. What complicates matters is that through the centuries, a crime could have been dealt with in manorial courts, summary courts or church courts. There were even special courts for the army and for the admiralty. Your ancestor's offence therefore leaves a paper trail but that might run through a dark forest rather than a sunlit path.

Offences
First be clear about this distinction:

Summary and indictable
A summary offence may be tried by a magistrate only, whereas an indictable offence has to be tried before a jury. This relates also to the definitions of *felony and misdemeanour*: a felony, until the Criminal Law Act of 1967 was a serious offence, and before 1870, it meant that the convict would forfeit all lands and chattels, and often being sentenced to death as well. A misdemeanour was a less extreme offence, usually tried summarily.

Medieval Courts

In the centuries between the Anglo-Saxon kingdoms and the first assizes (courts on a national circuit held by the King's travelling justices) before there were proper courts there was a system of blood-price and hue and cry. The local hundreds, groups of people, would be responsible for law and order in their community. More serious crimes were dealt with by ordeals of water or fire. But with the manors and the bishoprics came manorial and church courts and after them, in 1361, the justices of the peace, the magistrates.

The records of these early courts are in Latin, but many have been translated by county record societies and are available in book form. For more serious offences- felonies – the most common sentences are fines and outlawry. Fines gave the sovereign money, whereas a hanging yielded him nothing. As for outlaws, they were hounded by everyone and their fate was almost always a bloody death, with all their possessions forfeit.

The powerful bishops could and did hang felons, so most areas, as may be seen on old maps, had gallows dotted around, some secular and some ecclesiastical. All this was before the reforms of the fourteenth and fifteenth centuries when 'The King's Peace' was more thoroughly preserved in a series of statutes.

Early Modern Courts

Throughout the centuries, small misdemeanours were dealt with quickly and efficiently in manorial court leets or other kinds of summary courts. As Peter King has written in his study of these courts: 'In almost every county there were also many magistrates who heard individual cases alone in their homes' and he notes that, 'an increasing number of both administrative and legal functions were passed down to them by the legislature...' We can have a glimpse at this kind of record if we look at *The Justicing Notebook of Edmund Tew, Rector of Bolden*, published by the Surtees Society. In his journal we find entries such as these:

1763
November 15^t. Granted general warrant against Isabel Reed of Shields, fruiterer, for defrauding.... Of ditto widow a pair of shoes. Agreed.
22nd Granted a search warrant against George Turner of Jarrow, farmer, for concealing timber in his outhouse of Robert Waynman of North Shields. Agreed.

For various areas of the North East and the North West of England, the publications of the Chetham Society and the Surtees Society provide a great deal of details of offenders in those areas in the Early Modern period, and in fact, the court leet records of Manchester for the sixteenth century gives a very substantial account of such legal practices. A court leet was a type of summary court, probably coming from the Old English verb *gelethian,* to assemble together. Manchester ancestors who transgressed even in these very minor ways can be located in the records and indexes.

These sources show just what a huge amount of everyday law was handled by the magistrates and the justices presiding at leets and petty sessions. The topics coming before the sessions could be anything from petty theft to homicide, but much of the time was taken up with sorting out people from other parishes who had come into another parish, or with lack of payment to constables. Often is was a matter of debating issues such as who should repair a certain bridge or what should be done with a deserter. With every day that passes, more and more of these texts are made available, and are often found in university libraries as well as in local archives.

Debtors, Deserters and Drunks
Summary courts and magistrates' courts were not all about dealing with robbers and killers. They also heard cases of insolvency and other marginal crime.

Debtors
Debt cases in history will involve access to and scrutiny of civil court records. Obviously, this misfortune is linked to credit and to individuals or families living beyond their means. The general newspapers and trade papers listed debtors and bankrupts. These unfortunate people found themselves living in awful gaols and houses of correction, and the prison reformer, John Howard, estimated that in 1779 there were 2,000 debtors in the gaols.

The simplest way to grasp the lives and destinations of debtors is to look at the main gaols in London in the eighteenth century: the Fleet, the Marshalsea and Whitecross Street. The defining characteristic of these places was that they were businesses. For instance, the house of correction at Northallerton, the oldest prison still in the Prison Service Establishment, began in the 1780s with a division of debtors and prisoners on sentence or on remand. Vagrants, debtors and ruffians were together (male) but the women were kept in separate accommodation. It was essentially a factory:

all work was logged in a daily labour book, giving the amount of work done, and these figures were then transferred into quarterly books, with all costs monitored.

By 1520 there were 180 offences that were punishable by a prison term. Debt actions figured in this as results of civil actions, the result of one citizen prosecuting another for debt, and then prison followed, not as a punishment but to make sure that the debtor was under supervision until such time as he could gather some funds and pay the debt. In the Fleet, in the 1770s, there were 242 debtors, and they lived there with their families. In *Little Dorrit*, Dickens presents a picture of life in the Marshalsea, the prison where his father, John, had been imprisoned for debt.

Cases of debts had been handled at the Court of Requests through the centuries until the Small Debts Bill of 1845 when county courts were established. As Charles Nicholl has recently shown in his book, *The Lodger*, Shakespeare was involved in a claim at this court – giving evidence on 11 May, 1612 in the lawsuit Belott v Mountjoy. Nicholl provides an interesting sidelight on historical research when he notes that the first historian of the case had to work with uncalendared bundles of papers at the Court of Requests archives in 1909.

*

Debtors at the Great Yarmouth Bridewell, 1818
'The apartments for the debtors are mostly above stairs and are in a tolerably Good state. There are about nine beds for master debtors and three for common Debtors: but in one room appropriated to the latter class, 21 feet by 12 eight or ten have slept at one time.

Debtors from the Court of Requests have been Sent in contiguous thereto..... I was told that the prisoners were kept shut up In their cells all the day as well as during the night...'

The Small Debts Bill of 1845 brought in the very sensible measure of securing the payment of judgement debts not exceeding £20. It enabled a creditor to apply to any court for the recovery of the debt and made county courts and any other court for the recovery of small debts a part of the system

The Modern period, Victorian to the end of Assizes

In the 1850s, Charles Dickens edited a journal called *Household Narrative*; in this publication we find summary reports under the heading 'Law and Crime' and a glance at the 1854 collected volumes has reports from these courts: a court-martial; Lincolnshire assizes; the London Guildhall; Bow Street magistrates' Court; Marlborough Street Police Court; a coroner's inquest at Hunslet, Leeds, and the Court of Queen's Bench sitting in Dublin. Criminal ancestors were present in all these locations, with crimes ranging from 'stealing a bit of velvet riband' to a case of 'wilful murder against Joseph Baines' who was charged with killing his wife. Such is the proliferation of courts and trials in British history and the family needs to find a way through this labyrinth.

The Georgian and Victorian years saw first a rise in capital crimes, up to c. 1820, and then a gradual dominance of police courts and magistrates courts to sort out less serious offences, while quarter sessions and assizes dealt with almost everything. But in 1861 the Offences Against The Persons Act reduced the number of capital offences to just four, and there was a gradual move towards having a process of criminal appeal, so that in 1907 a court with that role was created.

The assizes continued until 1971, when they were superseded by Crown Courts.

A Check-List
Assizes:
These were held from the 13th century until 1971. The system had its origins in which two judges would hold the sovereign's court twice a year. These tried criminal cases and civil. From 1550 records provide details of such offences as homicide, infanticide and major theft. Before 1733 assize records are in Latin and the main records are indictments (statements of charges); depositions (written evidences) and gaol books or minutes (lists of accused persons and summaries of cases) heard. If there are no assize records surviving, then there are sheriffs' assize vouchers, located at THA E389 and also, for writs, the King's Bench records. The King's Bench.

The Gentleman's Magazine published details of the assize circuits, such as this entry from the 1819 issue: 'Spring Circuits, 1819: Norfolk, Lord Chief Justice Abbott and Baron Graham: Aylesbury, March 4, Bedford March 10, Huntingdon March 13, Thetford March 20, Bury St Edmund's March 26.'

Quarter Sessions
These were where the justices of the peace sat in judgement, from their creation in 1285. By the 18th century these 'bench' meetings had a massive work load.

Petty Sessions

These were summary courts, dealing with all kinds of minor matters, normally with two magistrates sitting. From 1828 quarter sessions were empowered to form county petty sessions. Increasingly in the Victorian period, police courts took over the handling of everyday criminal proceedings. The simplest way to understand what these were and how they worked is to search in the Times Digital Archive for such as 'Hull Police Court' and study some examples.

In addition to these, other courts relevant to your research will be these (all will occur in the following case studies):

Coroners' courts: The first hearing for responses to deaths, suspicious or otherwise. These were often held in public houses.

Courts martial: a military court, where your criminal ancestor may have had his case heard, rather than in a criminal court.

Church courts: These have various names and have unusual jurisdiction, such as the Court of Arches, whose records are at Lambeth Palace. But church Consistory courts would often sit in cathedrals and hear cases within the Bishop's jurisdiction.

For criminal proceedings this was the structure:

Magistrates / summary courts/ petty sessions-assizes- appeal courts (limited and for the wealthy) - High Court of Justice – Court of Criminal Appeal (for all since 1907) – House of Lords. Notice that appeal courts are added here to the normal main three courts. If your ancestor committed a serious crime, the appeal may have gone to the very top, as in rare cases of condemned convicts who appealed for a *respite* (a pardon or commutation of sentence).

Where to Find the Main Court Records:
Quarter sessions records: at your local CRO. Check the web site of the archive first, then visit and use the index: this is extremely useful, summarising the material in the holdings.
Assize records: See TNA key for Criminal Trials 1559-1971 and Assizes, Welsh, 1831-1971. Click on 'assize records' at the TNA website
Old Bailey Sessions papers for 1674-1913 are searchable online. See www.oldbaileyonline.org
King's Bench (the highest criminal court) see TNA reference at KB2 for 1682-1985
Police Courts The quickest search is to use The Times Digital Archive and enter the name and date

Disputes and Hearings in the Ecclesiastical Courts

In 1704 a Yorkshireman called John Thompson went with some friends to a local tavern in Rothwell and there he met a man called William Clarkson, who began to shadow him around the place, calling him 'a... and a rogue.' Clarkson was clearly boiling over with indignation and hatred. He went on to accuse Thompson of being a thief, a sheep-stealer and a coiner.' Thompson had plenty of witnesses to this speech, which was spoken with malice, and so he brought a suit against him in an ecclesiastical court at York.

That case would be known as a 'cause' in such a court, and the kind of law theorised and applied was a mix of common, canon and civil law. In other words, the ecclesiastical courts, when looked at from the standpoint of the mainstream criminal courts, are 'like a foreign country... they do things differently there' as L P Hartley famously said.

Your ancestor may well have found him or herself standing at one of these courts, and most likely the offences in question would have been more moral than criminal acts. But that is not the full story. Sorting out the different courts and how they worked is a definite challenge, but the records are solid and fascinating, dealing with many topics from fornication to slander. In fact, in the complex map of all English courts in the legal system, in certain instances, the ecclesiastical courts could feed into the system at the level of the high courts of justice – the superior courts – rather than being organically part of the inferior courts, the magistrates and quarter sessions courts in the criminal law.

For instance, in the Victorian age, certain matters that arose at the Court of Arches at Lambeth Palace, involved such allegations as, when in fact the action was for restitution of marital rights. There may well have been such offences (which, if tried in a criminal court, would have been very serious indeed).

Origins

The ecclesiastic courts began in the tenth century with a law that stated: 'the bishop of the shire and the aldermen in the hundred courts expound both things, as well as the law of God, as the secular law.' Later, after the sixteenth century Reformation the practice developed whereby courts were held by the bishop, the dean and chapter, and by the archdeacon. The latter held the court for the diocese and so had the most business to do. The bishop of each diocese would have a 'visitation' in his first year in office and then every three years following. For the archdeacons, their courts would be annual, but would be suspended if the bishop arrived for a visitation. The hearing would be presided over by a chancellor, and the final decision was made by an appointed person such as a lawyer- the official principal.

In addition to these courts, there were also 'peculiars' – these were locations which were beyond the jurisdiction of the bishop, and these could be held under the guidance of a wide assortment of bodies and individuals. Records for the peculiars are not necessarily substantial nor even complete in sequences or collections, but Anne Tarver has researched the Lichfield courts and has shown that there are very useful records there.

The records of these church courts are called Act Books, but these may also be termed Courts Books. A person would be in the position of the registrar to such courts, and the work he did would be the source of the records, hence the scanty and unpredictable nature of these archives.

Later, the term 'consistory court' came into use. The word was used of all the church courts except for the Court of Arches. This Lambeth court was the highest court – acting as an appeal court in fact. The consistory court and archdeacons' courts would be held on sacred ground, within the church establishment. The placing of the court furniture would be such that the hierarchy of those present would be paramount, so that there would be a high seat for the archdeacon for example, and the seating for those involved would have a boundary structure, making a tight, well defined court area. There was plenty of business in the courts: in 1575 the Archbishop of York in his visitations across his diocese brought 1,200 defendants into the courts.

Business and Administration

The church courts dealt with the proving of wills and disputes over tithes but they also had powers in moral matters, and they dealt with straightforward issues such as non-attendance as well as such difficult and sensitive areas of human life and relationships as, adultery, and slander. Even blasphemy would be sometimes heard and punished, and it must be recalled that a man was hanged in Scotland in the eighteenth century for that offence. Naturally, there was often violent and resentful feeling against locals by others, and there was always the chance that accusations were merely personal. But in earlier times, the church and churchmen had immense power and respect of course.

Five Types of Causes

There were five areas of activity in these courts: the first was that relating to parish and clergy relationships, and this could include sexual deviance. The formal term for these was *Officium Dominum*, shortened to OD, and it is easy to see why the phrase 'bawdy courts' was often used to define these hearings. Sometimes there would be very serious matters such as applications to bury suicides, but generally the majority of causes heard were for various categories of outside marriage. An interesting comparison arises when we reflect on the frequent occurrence of 'rough music' in which the local community would make their disapproval of immoral behaviour known by creating an unholy row beneath the bedroom of an adulterer for instance, and the punishment meted out in the church courts. The punishment was basically public shaming, such as apologising before the congregation and a formal statement of that penance. The transgressors may even have been ordered to wear white sheets over themselves at church service.

Fundamentally, the punishments given in this context relate to the punishments of public humiliation in the criminal courts, at petty sessions, when the stocks and pillory were used, or there was a public whipping ordered (usually done by the town hangman). These are all varieties of punishment intended to apply actions leading to conformity and acceptable behaviour within a defined community, usually the parish of course.

The second area was the matter of defamation. These involved public insults of course, such as that suffered by Mr Thompson in Rothwell. Arguments related to adultery would naturally lead to name-calling and slander in the open. Terms used relating to bawdy occupations were common, as is often evident in Shakespeare's plays when characters fling insults at each other.

Of course there were matrimonial causes, the third category. Contracts of marriage were extremely important: the business of estates, inheritance, property and so on, all linked to marriage and acceptable forms of being affianced. Women wanting the conjugal rights of property tended to be a common hearing; sometimes these would lead to appeal, as in the Court of Arches, or even seep into the equity courts within the main civil legal system.

Before 1857, the only way of having a divorce was by Act of Parliament, so for most people, who had not the financial resources to do this, the only option was to turn to the church courts to request a legal separation. That would generate alimony payments and there would be no marrying again for either party until one spouse died.

The fourth material related to tithes: when people did not pay their tithes, and so vicars would have the relevant parties in the archdeacon's court usually, for redress. This interaction of clergy and parishioners was really a matter of accepted duty and tact, but it could be handled with a human touch, as the vicar and diarist Francis Kilvert showed: he writes of a tithe dinner in 1878:

'Today was the tithe audit and tithe dinner to the farmers, both held at the Vicarage. About 50 tithe payers came, most of them very small holders, Paying as little as 9p. As soon as they had paid their tithes to Mr Heywood In the front hall they retired to the back hall and regaled themselves with Bread, cheese and beer...'

Finally, there were probate issues. People might be ordered to produce a probate inventory to verify that the proper probate testamentary measures had been taken; then, in causes where there was no person acting for probate, executors would have to appear in court. There were also the problems associated with people dying intestate; if the named executors could not be found or did not act, then there was more court business required.

The situation might arise in which a surviving spouse remarried quickly, and so there would be probate to wind up, and a secondary one if that person who wed again then died. In the Georgian and Victorian periods the life expectancy was not what it is now of course, and the Grim Reaper was a frequent caller. The new spouse of the person who had remarried and then died would be left with a secondary probate. It comes as no surprise that Charles Dickens and other writers found these dilemmas in which the human emotions clashed with legal problems and 'the law's delay' set in.

More Stormy Emotional Situations

Of course, the church courts were useful in other ways for people with other marital problems. If one person desperately needed a marriage to be invalid, then they could turn to the church rather than to civil courts; in the centuries leading up to the modern age of enlightenment in these matters, marital cruelty, for example, was very hard to prove. But cause of this kind in the courts could be about various problems: there might be non-consummation of the marriage, or there may have been a lack of consent. In the early eighteenth century, for instance, there was a lucrative business between London and Ireland which involve abduction and forced marriage. In some instances there may even have been the contentious and uncertain area of lunacy – which had to be proved to be the case before the marriage, not afterwards.

THE COURTS IN ORDER OF STATUS

Prerogative Courts – superior courts with power over those below
The Bishop's Court
Archdeacons' Court
Peculiar Courts (held by dean and chapter or manorial lords)
 (the Bishop's Court was sometimes called a consistory court but the term covered both a Bishop's and a Dean's court also.)
Appeal Courts: Process was ultimately to the House of Lords

A Basic Guide to Essential Terminology

Act Books The formal records of the courts

Archdeacon A senior clergyman with an area of authority given by his bishop.

Cause papers Cases – heard by the chancellor of the diocese

Consistory Court This became a general term for all church courts, though it was first used of a bishop's court only.

Officium Dominum (OD)The office of the judge – a cause related to the clergy and their parishioners

Peculiar A location technically outside the jurisdiction of the bishop.

Presentment A statement made on oath in church court (or made by a churchwarden) at the time of a visitation.

Visitation The period spent by the bishop in the diocese when his courts are to be in session.

*

Three Case Studies

Geils v Geils 1847-48

The first case was heard at the Court of Arches, beginning as a suit for restoration of conjugal rights and commencing at the consistory court in Salisbury. In 1845, Mrs Geils, 'being unmindful of her marriage vow, withdrew herself without just cause from the house and society of her husband, and had refused to return and cohabit with him. 'The cause for this restoration went to the higher court and in the course of a long and complex trial, what happened was a truly astounding example of 'washing the dirty washing in public' with all kinds of serious allegations being made by both parties.

This extract from the court report will show how hostile matters became: *'Mr Geils treated his wife with indifference, which soon degenerated into great and increasing harshness… at all times preferring the society of his own relations to that of his wife.. that within the first two years of their marriage she had five severe miscarriages, and was in a state of ill health during the whole of such period… when quarrelling he would abuse her in coarse terms, calling her "Devil " and the like…'*

In fact, this led to severe criticisms levelled at the Court of Arches by *The Times*, which printed a response to the Geils case after the judge had lost his self-control: 'The Court of Arches has long been looked upon as an anomaly; it bids fair now to be regarded as a nuisance.' (Jan.28 1848). It emerged that Mr Geils, the plaintiff, had boasted of his friendship with the judge 'as a great element in his success.' The judge was Sir Herbert Jenner-Fust.

A Probate Problem for Cobbett's Son 1835

The great radical and writer William Cobbett brought a great deal of business before the church courts. There had been a family quarrel in 1833, two years before his death on 27 June, 1835 and the only beneficiary in his will was his son William, who had remained faithful and lived with his father in the last years. Cobbett had other children and a wife and he made no provision for them.

The family row broke out in a church court and then went to the Prerogative Court of Canterbury, a superior court within the High Courts of Justice echelons. There the will was proved, and the son

William agreed to accept the administration of his father's effects. It was stated that 'The testator bequeaths the copyright of his works and all his other property to his eldest son, William.'

Cobbett's biographer, Richard Ingrams, wrote that 'The Cobbetts successfully repressed nearly all evidence of the quarrels, and it was not until 1982, with the publication of George Spater's biography, that the full story was revealed.'

Elizabethan Measures against an idle Churchman 1599

This is a very typical example of the kinds of problems faced by the churchwardens. They had to deal with all kinds of local irritations and arguments, always with a moral issue at the core, and in many cases the aim of the court was to satisfy the parishioners with regard to problems which the constables or magistrates would not be bothered to act upon.

In 1599 a 'clerk' (parson) in Chipping Ongar lived idly'; without serving any cure' and the churchwardens stated that this was 'contrary to the articles and laws ecclesiastical.'

The court record states:

Item: we present him for not receiving the sacrament in our church for three quarters of this year, of purpose going out of the town every communion to avoid it.

Item: we present him to be a malicious, contentious and uncharitable person & a railer of our minister and of most of the inhabitants that do profess religion, calling them heretics, hypocrites such as he hath ever & in every place detested etc.

Item: we present him for his open absence from prayers on the Sabbath days, in contempt of our minister & his usual departure out of church, at such time as he cometh before the people be dismissed, contrary to the articles.

This is a perfect example of a **presentment**: a term used in law for the statement of an accusation before a grand jury in criminal law until 1933. But it was a term also used in the church courts, describing exactly what the paper did – *present* a list of charges.

The End of the Church Courts

In 1857 the government took over the administration of divorces. From that date the court concerned with this subject was the court of Divorce and Matrimonial Causes. After 12 January, 1858 wills, which had formerly been proved by the church were then proved in the context of civil procedure. Wills were held after that by the Court of Probate, and there is a detailed index to wills at the *National Probate Calendar*. This may be consulted at TNA, at the Guildhall Library or at the Society of Genealogists.

The Difficulty of Finding Sources

As Paul Carter wrote in his book, Sources for Local Historians: 'Church court records are potentially invaluable but are virtually unexplored.' The main reason for this is arguably the fact that they are quite intricate and complicated; the vocabulary has to be absorbed gradually, as the terms used are not always those used in the mainstream criminal courts. An important point to grasp here is that the process through the courts relates to the class and wealth of the people involved. For most cases, the issues were related to everyday moral matters, but if wealthy middle or upper class people were in court, then it would be possible for the whole affair to escalate (as with the Geils example) and it may even have been heard in a superior court before a closure was reached.

The church courts and their business give the historian a very special insight into social and personal life through the centuries; they always provide highlights into the broader social context, whether that be the manor or the family ideology as a particular point in time. One important contrast here is to note that until the 1890s, in the criminal courts, the accused could not speak for him or herself, so the records there do not give us that insight; whereas in the church courts, a great deal is provided regarding the person in question.

THE LEARNED WIGS CONFER

The Crown Cases Reserved, 1848-1907
In 1883 a certain Jane Clark was indicted at Durham Assizes for a 'nuisance' which was in this case 'exposing the body of a child in a public highway'. This was a Common Law misdemeanour, and Judge Denman told the jury, 'I am not at all sure that this case is free from doubt in point of law.' Denman finally announced that he had consulted his fellow judges and he arrived at the decision that Jane had indeed committed an offence under the Common Law. She was sentenced to six months in prison.

On the surface this appears to be a hard, emotionless decision, inflicting a tough sentence on a poor women who was probably half-mad with poverty and anxiety. Her mental health is not in question, it seems. The decision rested on 'a point of law.'

What had happened when Denman consulted his fellow judges was that they had met to consider 'crown cases reserved.' This meant that a group of the best legal minds in the land would meet at Westminster Hall and help the judge to sort out a fair result. It was intended to handle cases heard at the quarter sessions, and so the variety of cases considered would be diverse and would range in their seriousness a great deal.

This was in effect a measure to deal with matters that later would be part of an appeal process, but in 1848, when the reserved cases were first heard, there was no court of criminal appeal: that came much later, in 1907.

The 1848 Enquiry

This meeting of the 'learned wigs' had its genesis in the 1848 Criminal Law Amendment Bill, and in the official enquiry and report on the bill as it was being created, we have a fascinating insight into how and why the crown cases reserved was established. For family historians, the records of the discussions may offer a source for finding ancestors which is out of the structure of the mainstream courts, so it is a useful legal resource for all kinds of historians and researchers.

In the government enquiry, Lord Campbell was in the chair and he interviewed Baron Parke and Baron Alderson, the legal minds principally behind the conception of the bill in 1848. This question and answer illustrate the need for the Crown cases Reserved:

Q *'What do you consider to be the present defect in the law on that subject? [points of law in criminal cases and ensuing doubt]*

A I consider the defect of the present law to be... that there is no proper mode of deciding doubtful questions of law that occur at quarter sessions.... In the next place I consider the present mode of deciding questions which are reserved by the judges is not so perfect as it might be; that the decision of these questions by the judges without delivering the reasons for their judgment causes the points so decided to be less entitled to the respect of the profession than they would be if reasons were given.'

The enquiry also looked at the difficulties in the same vein relating to trials heard at assizes and at the Central Criminal Court (which became the Old Bailey in 1834). That is, the problem was affecting all levels of criminal trials. The legal situation about complex points of law affecting decisions before 1848 was that there was no central authority, but 'Usage' was consulted and discussed. As Baron Parke told the enquiry: 'The fifteen judges, formerly the twelve judges, are merely the advisers of the judge who happens to try the cause; he refers to them for advice...'

When asked to explain further, he said, ' I conceive we are bound by the Usage, because it prevails back as far as our knowledge of law goes.'

In practical terms, when the new system was up and running, it created a workable option for some cases, many of which would only ever have had a consideration if the accused had paid for the costly process of an appeal, although Baron Parke did not agree with the argument that there should be a new establishment of a court of criminal appeal, saying that 'the inconveniences that would arise from it would greatly outweigh the supposed advantages.' But the case of *R v Camplin*, (1845) which took place before the new arrangements, shows that in effect the judge's discussions were still taking place effectively. This was a case of alleged rape.

Camplin worked hard to make a woman drunk and then took advantage of her, also striking her. The barrister for the defence, Ballantine, argued that 'To constitute rape there must be actual force, and actual resistance to that force. There must be an opposing will on the part of the person ravished.' But the panel of ten judges thought that Camplin's conviction was right and it was confirmed. The interesting point about this is that Baron Parke thought fit to add an explanation when the report was published, saying that the general consensus was that 'where the prosecutrix was made insensible by the act of the prisoner... when the prisoner must have known that the act was against her consent at the last moment at which she was capable of exercising her will, because he had attempted to procure her consent and failed, the offence of rape was committed.'

The conclusion of the 1848 enquiry, when the judges had been quizzed, was firmly on the side of the judge at the first trial being the one who decided on whether or not a decision would be reserved. As Baron Parke put it: ' ... I think it would be productive of great inconvenience if it were left to the uncontrolled will of the prisoner's counsel whether the point should be reserved or not, because in all cases where the punishment would be serious they would necessarily insist upon the point being reserved...' In other words, if a man was in the dock for murder and his fate hung in the balance over a fine point of law, he was entirely in the hands of the judge.

The Barons Parke and Alderton were keen to preserve the judge' status and power.

Playing a Part in Lawmaking
Naturally, if this new court was serving as some kind of alternative to an appeal process, and governed by the most experienced judges in the land, their decisions would form a significant part in fashioning law. The basis of this is in the reasons why questions were referred for consideration. One of the clearest examples of how the judges before 1848 had an influence on lawmaking was in the quite rare instance of a case from a court-martial being passed to them. This was *R v Dixon* (1797).

Eleven seamen on board the Saturn had been convicted of mutiny and condemned to die, but it was also ordered that their bodies be hung in chains, as was done across the land when gibbeting was decreed- where a killer's body would be left in a cage on a gibbet to set an example before the populace. The question was: could a court-martial have the power to issue such a decree? This was put before the twelve judges and they said that there was no such power. James Oldham, writing on how the judges in this context played a part in law-making, points out that it had been a thorny question, and that the king himself, via the privy Council, had sent the problem to the judges.

The work of the Crown Cases generally exercised a wide range of influences on all kinds of law. Behind this lay the tendency, since the middle years of the eighteenth century, for precedent to play a more prominent role in law-making. Although they were acting as a court of record, the great legal historian John Baker, wrote that ' their opinion was always acted on and if reported, would serve as a precedent for the future.'

Before the Court for Crown Cases reserved
What happened when there were challenging points of law before the Crown Cases Reserved existed? Traditionally, there was a general reluctance to overturn jury verdicts, but informal debates took place among the serjeants at Serjeants' Inn. A 'serjeant' was the term for the person at the highest level of the legal profession, and until 1846 they had exclusive privilege for an audience at the Court of Common Pleas. The degree is not now taken. For civil cases these were handled with more formality with a sitting *in banco*. This means 'on the benches' and there is a painting of such a sitting at the Royal Courts of Justice in the Strand, painted by Arthur Clay.

A case of infanticide illustrates what could happen In the early years of the nineteenth century there were many such cases: the usual outcome at that time was a death sentence. The fact is that young women, for all kinds of reasons (poverty, shame, stigma, mental illness) often took the life of a young child and tried to conceal the birth. One such woman was Jane Fletcher, who was tried and convicted, again before Sir Alan Chambre, at Hereford in 1803.

The sentence of death was given, and there was a crowd of other convicts in court at the time, so Chambre, being distracted by these other characters, omitted the part of the judgement that included the direction to have the woman's body dissected and anatomised. That was a common practice then, to give a felon's body to the medical students and so to give the final punishment of the victim's family having no body to bury.

It was only when Chambre was back in his judge's lodgings that he put this right, and he added the relevant section to the sentence on the calendar of prisoners. This was then taken but he still had to remedy this by speaking in open court. Cautiously, he respited Jane Fletcher's sentence until he could resolve that. Jane had four more days of life so that Chambre could consult with other judges on the matter. The great Lord Ellenborough was involved and in his chambers a group of learned men sat to consider the case; no decision was reached so there was an adjournment. Jane would then have three more months in prison awaiting her fate.

The judges met again on 10 June and they were again divided: these were the most learned and experienced legal minds of that time, and at that meeting in Serjeant's Inn were Ellenborough, Chief Justice, Lord Alvanley, the Chief Baron, and all the puisne judges (High Court judges). The only thing they all agreed on was that the omission could have been put right if Chambre had gone back to court after the adjournment, having the prisoner brought up from the court cell, and passing full judgement.

He had not done that, and the decision was that Jane Fletcher be 'reprieved generally.' She was in fact transported.

Another case of a point of law effecting a reprieve is that of Benjamin Pooley, whose crime was theft while employed by the Post Office. Pooley had taken a letter that had a draft for £200 in it. That meant that there were two counts against him: stealing the letter and then taking the draft. It was a felony on which he stood accused, a serious crime at any time. He was a post sorter and so was in a position of trust.

The draft was from one David Thomson in Maidstone, made out to his London bankers; the paper shown as evidence was unstamped. Chambre was to be a judge involved in much controversy just after this trial, principally after his involvement with the Lancashire Luddites, but he must have always recalled this strange affair. Although Pooley was found guilty, there was a technicality and that needed the consultation of other judges. This related to the original indictment: there was no stamp on the draft, so the question for the lawyers was whether or not this was acceptable as an indictment? The judges sat to deliberate: the Exchequer Chamber was the scene and for the crown there was the Lord Chief Justice, opposite a Mr Knowles who was later to be the Recorder of London.

After prolonged debate it was decided that the conviction was wrong; the indictment could not be called a 'bill' within the Act on which the offence was stipulated. That might have seemed as though Pooley would walk free, but no, he was then tried on a second charge, that of stealing a letter from the post. This was 1801, and that was a capital offence. He was found guilty and sentenced to hang, by Mr Justice Lawrence. But a report of the time explains why he never stood to receive the noose: '...but the court entertaining doubts whether the second section of the Act [7 Geo.IIIc.50 s.1]applied to servants of the post office, against whose misconduct the first section of that Act was intended to guard... the legislature did not conceive that the embezzling of a letter by those servants was a larceny and reserved the question for the opinion of the judges.'

On 2 May 1801, Mr Knapp spoke for Pooley and argued that, as the defendant was employed by the post office when he took the letter, he was exempt from the scope of the Act. Pooley was recommended to the crown for a pardon and walked from the court. Amazingly, on both counts, a technicality not specified or omitted from the text of the statute had made a pardon possible.

The Achievement
In the end, after the enquiry and report, the bill created the Court for Crown Cases Reserved. It was, in a way, a quiet revolution. It gave shape and structure to something that had been informal and rather whimsical at times. But it did provide a parallel function to appeal – a sort of self-generated checking system on the part of the assize or quarter session judge. The records stand as a little-known source for historians and family researchers whose ancestor's destiny after trial might not have been found in the mainstream criminal courts records.

Locating Records
Reading the collected cases of the Crown Cases Reserved today, one is struck by the importance of the minutiae in the wording of the law, and by the proliferation of precedent cases. At The National Archives, the King's Bench cases involving reserved discussion are at KB 30 and KB 31. At KB 30 there are the pleadings from quarter sessions and assizes.

At TNA reference CRIM 11 there are the records of the Old Bailey draft pleadings to the Crown Cases reserved court, and these cover the years 1848-1893. Orders for pleadings are at CRIM 12.

Further Reading
Stephen Charles Denison, *Crown Cases Reserved for Consideration* (William Benning, 1850)
Phil Handler, 'The Court for Crown Cases Reserved 1848-1908' *Law and History Review* February, 2011 pp. 259-288
Allyson N May, 'The Bench, the Bar and Crown Cases Reserved '*Law and History Review* Vol. 29 issue 01
James Oldham, 'Informal Law-Making in England by the Twelve Judges in the late 18th and early 19th Century' in Georgetown Law, The Scholarly Commons, 2011 See
www.scholarship.law.georgetown.edu/facpub/361/

British Parliamentary Papers: Royal Commission and select committee on the criminal law1847-79 (Irish University Press Vol. 61998)

    A useful way to understand the various courts in action is to use the Times Digital Archive and simply search one date-set of one type of court at a time. Maybe a first look at assizes for instance, over a decade, would give a clear idea of what they dealt with.

**

5

Other Criminal Sources
Reclaiming the Underclass

In the course of his work helping criminals in London in the 1890s, Thomas Holmes had some frightening experiences. On one occasion he wrote that he had gone into homes in which wives were shivering with fear and the children ran into safe hiding places as violent men threatened assault. He wrote: 'I have stood in front of these men and have been horribly afraid for my own safety, for with a poker or a hatchet in his hand, a man of this kind needs wary dealing. I know these men are mad but I know that no doctor will certify them as such...'

Holmes was one of the breed of unsung heroes who worked with the London underclass, trying to keep them from prison and a life of crime, years before there were professional probation officers, after the 1907 Act. He was born in Walsall in 1846, and he became an iron-moulder like his father; he worked in this trade until his early thirties, but he also spent time teaching the working classes, and after a serious accident, he was advised to apply to become a Police Court Missionary, and in 1885 he was successful, being attached to Lambeth Police Court. Holmes later wrote two books on his experiences, and in one of these he explains that he actually had a moment of epiphany which led to his new life.

If your ancestor was one of the thousands of poor and deprived Londoners who found themselves on the wrong side of the law in late Victorian Britain, then the chances are that one of the Missionaries worked with them and tried to help them.

The Police Courts

As the nineteenth century wore on, the volume of petty crime increased so much that the old system of what were called summary courts were increasingly organised and administered by the police rather than by legal professionals of various kinds. A massive influence on this accelerating volume of crime was drunkenness; so it is no accident that the Missionaries had their roots in the Temperance Movement. The Inebriates Act of 1898 made it possible for the courts to send drunks to a reformatory, and there were a number of homes for inebriates. But back in 1876, when the Police Court Missionaries idea was born, there was nothing to help the women or juveniles on the streets, scraping a living through selling anything from trinkets and matches to sex.

The human traffic passing through the police courts reflected the dismal failures of the affluent society of Victorian Britain, with its proud boast of wealth and progress, displayed in The Great Exhibition of 1851. Beneath the glamour and the expansion of Empire there was a growing class of people who found themselves before the bench for petty theft, hawking without a licence or prostitution. The police staff struggled to cope, and satires of the time, notably in *Punch,* revel in showing the swamping of the courts by the desperate and destitute. It is not difficult to imagine the chaos at the courts: a stream of people being brought in, and culprits in their dozens being loaded into the 'Black Marias' as they were shipped off to gaol; the Missionaries squeezed in and worked when and where they could.

Rainer and the Early Missionaries

It was in 1876 that a printer from Hertford called Frederic Rainer, who was working as a volunteer with the Church of England Temperance Society, saw this problem at the courts and decided to act. He gave five shillings to the philanthropists who were working in a small way to help offenders. The result was a tentative placement of two Missionaries in Southwark by the CETS. From there, a quiet revolution happened.

After that, two former Guardsmen, Batchelor and Nelson, became the first two Police Court Missionaries. One snippet of oral history suggests that their friendship included one episode in which Batchelor saved Nelson's life. Nelson was in the Coldstream Guards in 1861, and was discharged with good conduct in 1871. In 1877 he listed his activities, and these included visits to 438 homes, 293 attendances at police courts and 149 temperance pledges taken. He made 117 visits to prisons and saw 20 women sent to homes.

By 1880 there were eight full time Missionaries in place and homes were opened. By 1896 there were six 'mission women' in the team, and in London, these staff would interview women charged at court. Some of these were sent to an 'inebriates' home at Gratton Road. The service of the Missionaries was best summed up by Thomas Holmes, who said, 'Sir, I cannot carry Christ in parcels and distribute him. I can only do as I think He would have done... I give them myself.'

William Wheatley

There was someone else on the scene as well: William Wheatley. In 1887 Howard Vincent, ex Metropolitan police officer, saw through parliament his Probation of First offenders Bill; this did not establish probation officers, but brought about police supervision with Home Office backing. The most significant result of this bill was established because there was a stipulation that the offender being helped had to have a fixed 'place of abode.' In order that this could be fulfilled, Wheatley set up the St Giles Christian Mission. This was before the Police Court Missionaries could compete with this, and Wheatley began to collect and work with young men who had committed a first offence. In 1890, a reporter from *The Daily Graphic* looked into Wheatley's work. His report included this information:

'It was not always so obvious as it is now that there are more ways of reducing crime than by merely imprisoning criminals. A great deal is left to missions such as St Giles Mission to Discharged Prisoners, with which the names of Mr George Hatton and Mr William Wheatley have been so long associated.... The headquarters of the Mission are in Little Wild Street, one of those narrow and not so sweet-smelling streets leading off Drury Lane... But Mr Wheatley is usually found elsewhere, making his round of the prisons...'

Sacrifices and Support

The Missionaries went to extremes to help the fallen, the young ones destined to be on the police 'Habitual Criminals Register.' Thomas Holmes even offered his own house at times; he wrote that he dealt with alcoholics by giving them 'the shelter and protection' of his own home. Perhaps his most lengthy and heart-rending account of one of the offenders he worked with was that of Jane Cakebread. This poor woman, after a life of crime, died in Claybury Asylum and Holmes went to her funeral.

But this does not imply softness and indulgence: on the contrary, the usual statement made about the aims of probation- to 'guide, admonish and befriend' – hints at the toughness required as well as the sacrifice of time, labour and personal comfort. What was very much a help and support to the Missionaries, though, was the First Offenders Act of 1886. This made it easier to give the Missionaries the tasks of supervising young offenders who had been bound over; voluntary supervision was undertaken for a designated period.

All this needed cash of course. The support was not there without finance. A typical fund-raising effort was the concert given at Bycullah Athenaeum which raised a great deal of money. The Missionaries themselves were not particularly well paid – around £50 a year was average. But progress was made, and some of the main achievements of the Missions are very impressive, such as the boys' shelter at Bethnal Green in 1893 in which around twenty boys would stay and be supervised for several weeks. The achievements are best appreciated with a look at some figures: in the area of what is now Greater London, Missionaries visited over 5,000 homes, wrote over 3,000 letters and took over 2,000 pledges.

Outside London

The Missionaries existed in the provinces as well. In Cheshire for example, a Police Court Mission Committee was set up in 1894, created by a clergyman, the Rev. Cogswell. Within a year, the

Missionaries based in Chester had been involved in 240 court cases. The first Missionary employed was J C Porter, with a salary of £90 a year (doing much better than his London counterparts). The missions were then extended throughout the county, being established in Northwich, Altrincham and Stockport. The Chester Mission even extended its work as far as Wallasey and Broxton.

It has to be noted that not all the regions responded to opportunities to invest in this kind of probationary support: the understanding of the work done was slow to be disseminated, and of course, as it was always linked to church initiatives, there was perhaps a general feeling that things 'would just happen' left to the 'do-gooders.' In other words, there was not much in terms of organisational and corporate action to extend the work done in London in the early years. However, by 1900 there had been a definite change of gear in this respect and there were a hundred Missionaries in the country by then.

Missionaries in the Criminal Justice System

In the last decades of Victorian Britain, the results of the Industrial Revolution and of massive urban growth, together with huge scale immigration into London from Eastern Europe and Russia, meant that 'everyday' minor crime spread wider and went deeper: that is to say, as well as creating problems in the courts, this also added to penal issues such as the uncertainties about the prison system. In 1877 the prisons had been effectively nationalised and regimented, being run by military men. In terms of the efforts to provide help with rehabilitation, the emphasis was still on silence, reflection and hard work. Of course, until the end of the century, most local prisons had a full mix of ages, gender, and populations nurturing what was called 'contamination' – the first offenders being corrupted by old lags. Until the early Edwardian years, many gaols still had women offenders inside giving birth to children.

This wider view gives us an insight into exactly how important the Police Court Missionaries were in that social context. They reclaimed a large number of people who, without them, would have slipped into habitual crime as their only option, living in the sad and desperate underclass.

The 1907 Act

Speaking in Parliament in May 1907, Mr Herbert Samuel moved a second reading of the Probation of Offenders Bill, and he made a clear statement of its purpose:

' Its purpose was to enable Courts of Justice to appoint probation officers, and pay them salaries and fees, so that certain offenders whom the court did not think fit to imprison on account of their age, character or antecedents, might be placed on probation under the supervision of these officers...'

By the time of the Act, The London Diocesan Police Court Mission had clearly shown the way in this respect. The Annual Report for 1900 reflects on the nature of their work as well as the significant achievements. It lists the work done by thirteen Missionaries: they had even paid rent and lodgings for 343 people, and the total number of visits made by all the staff – to home and court – was 8,319.

There were concerns expressed about the new breed of probation officers – questions now raised which had never been raised against the 'amateurs.' Mr Stuart Worsley, Member for Sheffield Hallam, said in debate: ' What deduction was to be made from the liberty of the person who was placed under the control of a probation officer? ... Would the probation officers have the right of entry into a person's house, and if not, why not? Was the officer to have the right of following a person about the country?'

One might argue that this was a very English trait: to allow the good work to go on, with magnificent achievements, but then, when it was streamlined and 'official' and within a proper system, to start asking the important questions of both a legal and a moral nature.

But the Missionaries by this time were moving on. Thomas Holmes founded the Home Workers' Aid Association in 1904, and then in 1905 became a secretary with the Howard Association. Even near the end of his life he was still helping others, and with a communal aim: in 1910 he created Singholm at Walton on the Naze, a holiday home for women in the open air. Holmes, Nelson, Batchelor and the others achieved amazing things in their work in the byways of London crime, and an understanding of their work gives depth and texture to any family story that involves offenders and their rehabilitation.

The Story of Jane Cakebread

Thomas Holmes had special memories of some of his clients. The inebriate Jane Cakebread is one who never left his mind and imagination. He wrote of her, 'Fifty years I stood by and stood up for Jane Cakebread, and we became inseparably connected. She abused me right royally and her power of invective was superb. When she was not in prison she haunted my house and annoyed my neighbours.'

Jane told Holmes that he could be the heir to a fortune she never had, and at one time, she proposed to him. She tended to recite a section from the Book of Job if a quarrel was in progress among the drunks, and Holmes noted that she patronised him 'most graciously' when he gave her a change of clothing.

This is a kind of love story, a moving account of a professional relationship that became a strange friendship. Holmes went to her funeral and never forgot her, a drunken woman of the streets. He said that 'she bestowed her affections on me.' Her death in December, 1898 was reported in The Times: 'Jane Cakebread, who, according to official records, had been convicted 281 times for drunkenness, died on Saturday morning in Claybury Lunatic Asylum.' She had been remanded into Holloway prison 'for her state of mind to be inquired into' in January, 1896.

Timeline

1876 Frederic Rainer, working with the Church of England Temperance Society, donates five shillings to court missionary work.
1880 There were by this time eight missionaries in position.
1886 The Probation of First Time Offenders Act – this opened up similar missionary Work in regional courts.
1898 The Inebriates Act: giving court the power to retain inebriates in Reformatories
1907 The Probation of Offenders Act: missionaries were termed officers of the Court' – but then new probation officers were

appointed. This allowed courts to suspend punishment and create a recognizance to be supervised for a period of one to three years. (A recognizance is a bond of obligation made before a Court officer.)

Further Information
The most informative **printed primary source** comes from Thomas Holmes' two books:
Known to the Police (Arnold, 1900)
Pictures and problems from the London Police Courts (Arnold, 1902)
Also, Henry Mayhew, *London Labour and the London Poor* (1849-1850) published by Penguin Books, 1985

Archival material:
William Booth: Police Court Missionary, papers at London Metropolitan Archives Acc/1926/B/128/50-6
Cheshire and Chester Archives and Local Studies Service: reference: CPS. These refer to local Missionaries and the Police Court Committee

Books
For a full account of the growth and work of the Police Court Missionaries, see Martin Page, *Crimefighters of London*: A History and origins of the London Probation Service 1876-1965 (Inner London Probation Service, 1992).
George Mair and Lol Burke, *A Short History of probation* (Willan Publishing, 2010)

Further Essays
The Fair Sex and Unfair Laws

In one of the most influential tracts on English law, the great legal writer and lawyer Sir William Blackstone, wrote in his master work, *Commentaries on the Laws of England*, 'The husband and wife are one person in law; that is, the very being or legal existence of the women is suspended during her marriage, or at least is incorporated or consolidated into that of her husband...' Reading accounts of women offenders over the centuries, it is easy to see how this condition of being a mere 'chattel' had horrendous consequences. Blackstone's book was published in 1769, but if we go back to the earliest laws – those of the Anglo-Saxons – we see the source of inequality and the nature of women as possessions.

Before any national criminal justice system there were kings in various parts of the Anglo-Saxon areas and they made their own codes of law. At that time, crimes committed were put right by payments to the victims: damage to an eye cost fifty shillings, and to a toe nail just sixpence. Adultery and fornication were expensive hobbies; the church had a say in these matters of course. Through the Middle Ages, women as victims were in a tough position. The court rolls of Lincolnshire, for instance, in the twelfth century, show that savage attacks and rapes committed at night on lonely households were often punished merely with fines. Even in the great Magna Carta of 12 15, they could not accuse anyone of a murder except in the case of her husband being killed.

But as criminals, women generally appeared at the Quarter Sessions for their locality for offences relating to desperation and poverty. When they stood in the dock for serious crime, at assizes usually, a rare occurrence compared to men, the crimes were generally linked to sex, motherhood or what we would now think of as 'crimes of passion.'

In Court- from Thieves to Witches

If we look at the everyday Quarter Sessions reports from the Elizabethan period to the nineteenth century, we find sad instances of women involved in crime. In a hearing for Doncaster for instance, we have much robbery, theft, breaking and entering going on, and women are not often in the gangs: a widow called Katherine Booth broke into a house and stole a chest of goods, on her own. The offences were mixed in this respect. In October, 1637: one man stole a bible worth five shillings and a butcher of Cawthorne stole six wethers (sheep). Margaret Chambers stole a waistcoat, a petticoat and 'a pecke of oatemeale.' Petty theft was going on all the time, and it was often the usual opportunist business, as with two women of Brampton Byerley, who stole twelve sheaves of barley.

The 1637 sessions record a long list of crimes, and most were felonies, and so one possible punishment was death. Reading the account today, there is a deep sense of foreboding in the wording; sixteen men and two women were 'Put for good or ill upon the country, whereupon a jury was called.' We can imagine them all lined up before the twelve good men and true, waiting for their fate. The report goes on:

'. . . they were led to the bar by the sheriff and asked what they could say for themselves, why they should not have judgement of death according to the law for the felonies aforesaid whereof they

were convicted. They severally said that they were clerks and prayed for benefit of clergy to be granted them.'

What happened next was going on along the length and breadth of the land. The 'Benefit of Clergy' ruling meant that if a felon could read what was called the 'neck verse' –which they could claim on only one occasion, then they would be branded rather than hanged. The neck verse was the opening of the 51st psalm: 'Have mercy upon me, O God, according to Thy loving kindness: according to the multitude of Thy tender mercies blot out my transgressions.' The women as well as the men, were branded, in court.

When it came to witchcraft, it was a punishable offence from very early times, but the most celebrated cases were in 'epidemic' instances such as in the Elizabethan and Jacobean times, and again in the 1640s. By the end of the seventeenth century, attitudes changed, and the last execution in England was that of Alice Molland in 1684. The Witchcraft Act of 1736 made prosecutions for the offence illegal

Infanticide

Through the centuries, infanticide emerges as the one specifically female offence. It was a crime that only a mother could commit, and by a statute of 1624 the offender was defined as an unmarried mother. Court records (and execution records too) show a large number of sentences and hangings for this offence, though increasingly, courts took a more lenient view. In 1803 an Act was passed which made it essential for the prosecution to prove that the death was intended by the mother, not caused by natural illness. But it was not until the Infanticde Act of 1938 was it set apart from murder, taking into account the concept of post-natal depression. The phrasing was that mothers who may have taken the infant's life were 'disturbed by reason of not having fully recovered from the effects of giving birth.

Of course, abortion was linked to this, and that was not legalised until 1967; in the Edwardian and late Victorian years, with cases of baby-farming and back-street abortion, capital sentences were common. The related crime of 'concealing a birth' by a young mother was also very common throughout the Victorian period, and sentences could be severe, although more enlightened through the creation of reformatories and other institutions rather than prisons for these female offenders.

Prostitution

'The oldest profession' was often the province of the church courts – the so-called 'bawdy courts' which would have dealt with local cases. But this has always been very hard to regulate. In a publication on crime in London published in 1795, Patrick Colquhoun stated that there were 50,000 women in that trade.

For the Victorians, it became a problem needing attention when the health of the Empire's soldiers and sailors was at risk. The Contagious Diseases Acts of the 1860s made it possible to report a woman suspected of prostitution if she was working within ten miles of certain garrison towns. She had to report to a magistrate and then go to a hospital to be 'inspected.'

Murder

One of the most horrendous punishments a woman could suffer until the 1790s was burning at the stake – this was not for witchcraft however, but for petty treason. Until that time, if a man killed his wife, he had committed murder, but if a wife murdered her husband, the crime was petty treason (as opposed to high treason – against the state) and though he would be hanged, she would be burned. Common practice was for the executioner to be given money to strangle the poor victim before the fire was lit.

Of course, for the more everyday, usually relationship-related killing, convictions of women were few. After the 1860s executions for murder were less frequent and capital crimes were reduced to just four. Between 1868 (when public hangings were abolished) and 1955, there were 40 hangings of women, the last being Ruth Ellis. To illustrate the figures for men and women hanged: in the twentieth century there was a total of 865 executions, and of these only 18 were women.

On the whole, the history of women in the criminal law in Britain has been related to the national, fundamental struggle for rights such as the vote and for equality within marriage and in careers. Yet, it is astonishing that prison is still the standard punishment for women. In a report led by Baroness Corston in 2006, the conclusion was that most women who commit a crime should be dealt with in the community, and that a network of women's centres for these offenders be set up. The controversy goes on, and women's relation to crime, whether the offence is 'business' crime or an offence done in desperation, so in a sense, nothing fundamental has changed

A Domestic Tragedy : Mary Chapel

Mary Chapel was just nineteen, and in the domestic service of Colonel Surtees at Ackland, when she faced the judge and jury at York, and on a charge of infanticide: a similar predicament to that of Mary Thorp. Chapel's story is however, unlike Thorp's in one important respect – that she and the father were in love, and only parted because of the exigencies of hard times.

Mary courted a young man who was also in service, but as a contemporary account puts it, 'The young man to whom we have alluded became careless of his duties, excited reprehension and resolved at length, in that tumultuous year 1801, to take refuge in the army. The sequence of events that led to Mary's downfall is the material of literary tragedy. She and the young man walked out together and went to a local feast; her man had begged her to take some time off work for that. They had a good time, and of course, it was a rare opportunity for them to make love. Sure enough, that one fateful union led to her pregnancy, and in the way of grand opera or stage tragedy, her young man left for the wars in Europe and was never heard of again.

In June 1802 she gave birth to a girl. There appears to be a strange aspect to the story of the birth, as recounted in the trial report, because it is stated there that Miss Surtees, daughter to the Colonel, called for a doctor on the day in which Mary went into labour. Somehow, for months, the pregnancy is supposed to have been concealed from the master's family. Poor Mary was warned then of the dangers of 'destroying children' when in such a state of despair and disgrace. But the actual birth is the focus of attention for readers of the tale now, trying to understand what actually happened that Mary was charged with murder. It seems that she had a terrifyingly painful birth and, as the report at the time says, *'Some time after cries were heard... Half an hour after blood was seen on the bed; and on search, a new born female infant, dreadfully lacerated, was found between the bed and the mattress of an adjoining bed, its mouth was torn down to the throat, and its jawbone forced away,.'*

A Pontefract surgeon witnessed this and appeared in court to verify the medical condition of the child. He considered that there was some explanation, bearing in mind the girl's distraught state. Through modern eyes, we can see the potential delirium and even hallucination that attends on the stresses of birthing, but then it was almost impossible for temporary insanity to be ascertained and made convincing in court. The surgeon simply stuck to his opinion and the lawyer prosecuting admitted that the case described was improbable but not impossible.

The jury, then, were being ask to consider the fact that Mary had attacked the child in a fit of rage and despair, out of her wits, then hidden the corpse. Her statement in explanation was that she never meant the baby any harm. She said, 'I cannot recollect how or where I did it; if I did, God knows. I loved my child before I saw it.' She said again, 'I am a wretched woman. It was my child; I never meant it any harm.'

Fittingly, even the judge, a man seasoned to face this kind of lamentable situation, gave the sentence with some expression of emotion, after she had been found guilty of wilful murder. A week later she was hanged at York, but to the very end she never expressed her feeling that she was guilty; she insisted that she must have done the deed in a fit of delirium. Poor Mary was so tough in her last moments that she even endured a wait as there was a problem with the knotting of the rope. The massive crowds who usually gathered on the Knavesmire for a show and entertainment were not in such a mood that day: they were subdued, and a report from the time says that Mary '... died without a struggle, amid the audible sobs of the multitude.'

What made the whole business so difficult in court was that she had evidently killed the baby with her own hands; there was no evidence of any weapon being used. As a writer twenty years after the event noted, 'Those who know the dreadful weakness attendant upon an accouchement, especially in the moment after the delivery, will see how impossible it is that she could have forced the jawbone away after the birth.' Either the child was killed in an agonising part of the birthing, or — and this is a long shot- some other person, wanting to help the girl in her desperate situation, did the killing for her.

Further Information

Books:
Geoffrey Abbot *Lipstick on the Noose* Summersdale, 2003
Angela Brabin *The Black Widows of Liverpool* Palatine Books, 2003
D'Cruze, Shani *Crimes of Outrage: Sex, Violence and the Victorian Working Woman* UCL Press, 1998
Sian Rees *The Floating Brothel* Review, 2001
James Sharpe *Witchcraft in Early Modern England* Pearson, 2001
Susan Steinbach *Women in England 1760-1914* Orion, 2005
Stephen Wade *Yorkshire's Murderous Women* Pen and Sword, 2007

Websites:
www.capitalpunishment.org/femhang.html
www.murderfiles.com
www.womenshistory.about.com

Records and Archives

The National Archives has a new database for women prisoners, labeled the Female Prisoners Licence Files PCOM4, arranged by licence number.

Suffragette court and prison records: at TNA: CAB 41/32/62; CAB 41/34/8; MEPO 2/1410 and HO 45/10645/209446.

For murder cases, executions are most easily traced at The Female Hanged 1868-1955, and this is at www.capitalpunishmentuk.org

Other common offences will be in the records along with all general criminal archives at the County Record Offices, but for Victorian to modern offences, search The Times Digital Archive, or search by name at Black Sheep Index which has all press reports by name and date: blacksheepindex.co.uk. For a small fee, a copy of the press report featuring your ancestor may be ordered.

Medieval and Early Modern Records: use county record publications first: names are listed in indexes here, and name searches in plea rolls at TNA or in CRO indexes will be a useful first step.

A Timeline of Women and the Law in great Britain

1736 Witchcraft Act made prosecutions for witchcraft illegal
1790 Petty treason, in which a servant killed a master or a wife killed a husband, was converted into murder. This meant that no

longer would a woman who murdered her husband be subject to death by burning, rather than death by hanging, which would have applied if a man killed his wife.

1860 The first model prison was constructed at Millbank. A separate system for Men and women was established.

1861 The number of capital offences were reduced to just four, and the death penalty for attempted murder was abolished.

1864,1866 and 1869 Contagious Diseases Acts: forcible inspection of prostitutes

1870 Married Women's Property Act allowed a woman to keep property gained after marriage

1938 The Infanticide Act states that if a woman is to cause the death of her child by 'wilful act or omission' but does so when it can be demonstrated that at the time the balance of her mind was 'by her not having recovered from the effect of giving birth to the child' then the offence would be infanticide, not murder, and so would be a variety of manslaughter.

THE AMERICAN GANG

On a cold autumn day in 1872, Inspector John Shore of Scotland Yard was walking along the Strand in London, with Bill Pinkerton, of the famous detective agency that never slept. Shore was a young man, in his early twenties, and he had started his police career in Bristol before moving to the big city. His rise was meteoric: in a few years not only had he reached the rank of Detective Sergeant, but he had a nick-name: John Blunt. This was stuck on him because of his direct approach to dealing with people. As for Pinkerton, he was visiting his brother Robert, who was the representative of the

Agency, based in London and living at the grand Cecil Hotel on the Strand, next to the great Savoy.

As they moved along, chatting about the crime-wave of the day- footpads and very nasty robber gangs preying on late-night theatre-goers and innocent tourists who wandered off the safer sidewalks of the metropolis, Pinkerton's gaze landed on some familiar faces: he saw the brothers George and Austin Bidwell, along with their friend George Macdonnell. The sighting was duly noted, and by this time, a certain level of sophisticated detective communication had been established in Britain. Her Majesty, Queen Victoria had a state with professional detectives created exactly thirty years before this walk in the Strand. In 1842, the bobbies in uniform had been supplemented by the plain-clothes sleuths.

Inspector Shore was given the low-down on the young Americans; George was thirty-three and Austin just two years younger, and they were already confident in their expertise as con-men. George Macdonnell was the youngest in the party, at merely twenty-two years of age at that time, when the detective knew him. The Bidwells had already become acquainted with the Wall Street culture and George was well connected, his parents being a respected Boston family. His father had financed a business venture for his son, George, and that had failed, so the young man was despatched to Europe, where perhaps Shakespeare's words apply: 'to follow such winds as do blow about the world/further from at home/ where small experience grows' But then, giving this another spin, we might suspect that Mr Macdonnell senior wanted respite from a son whose brain was ticking 24/7 with questionable schemes for enrichment, often on the wrong side of the law.

Word was circulated across the city, giving a suitable warning that it was likely that some scheme of forgery or fraud was possibly imminent, and that all banks should take special care when dealing with new clients.

However, poor naïve London was about to be ripped off on a very large scale. The young men seen across the Strand were not only clever and devious criminal minds: they were also able to transform, to shape-change as adeptly as any tragic actor, and this, combined with the skills of forging official documents, was to offer a challenge to the banking system at the very heart of the world's greatest Empire. The spirited young rakes, wrapped in their overcoats that autumn day, were actually more dangerous to the status quo than an outfit armed with guns and knives. They carried the profoundly effective threat of charm on the surface with the ethics of a shark beneath that smooth exterior.

For the police officers at that time, there were certainly moments of high drama and major crime as well as of the daily grind of larceny and assault. In 1864, for instance, seven pirates were convicted for the murder of the captain of the ship, *The Flowery Land*. They were hanged in front of Newgate prison, and as they had committed the crime within the jurisdiction of the Admiralty, meant that the new City Commissioner, Colonel Fraser, attended to the security. No less than five hundred City police were on duty that day; five of the pirates were being hanged and such a group hanging had not taken place since 1828. *The Times* reported favourably on the City police: *'...it was apprehended that an enormous crowd would assemble, and the sheriffs, with Colonel Fraser...made such arrangements as appeared commensurate with the occasion for the maintenance of law and order and the protection of life. Happily in the result these were most effective and well suited to the emergency. Colonel Fraser had the whole of the available space from which a view of the execution could be obtained... intersected by strong barriers.'*

Only four years before Pinkerton's walk with Shore, public executions had been abandoned, and capital offences were reduced to four; but the wind of change was bringing the kinds of threats to security and the established order which work unseen, generated by the intellect rather than the force of sheer muscle. The young Americans were to create the kind of mayhem that the new dimensions of 'clever crime' were to bring before the forces of law.

By 1870 there were 30,000 police officers in England and Wales; but the CID was a thing of the future – not established until 1878. The Special Branch came in 1884 to deal with security matters. The former was partly because 'white collar' crime was emerging more threateningly, and the latter because the Fenian Irish had a tendency to bomb London. Terrorism arrived, and it was out in the streets: bank fraud, however, was doing its deadly work in silence, along business systems and in and out of accounts and credit transactions. In many ways, the new versions of white collar crimes were more challenging to social stability than bombs, and the American Gang were to show, in 1873, that a pillar of the establishment could be duped and robbed on a massive scale.

He had that kind of restlessness that troubles rebels like a pain around an old scar, the kind that nothing but newness, fresh starts, open roads, will ease. It was of the robust intellectual kind: the fidgets were cerebral and the hunger for another kind of challenge was going to gnaw at him all his life, but in 1872 George Macdonnell was young, eager and ambitious. He had no specific aims and objectives, but he would sense the right kind of challenge when it came along, like a prairie dog sniffing the wind. It would have to be something on a grand scale. Morality was never in the reckoning either: the challenge could as easily have been to walk across Siberia as to steal the Mona Lisa.

He was tall, hearty and restless; he found standing still to be an impossibility. George breezed through his studies and demonstrated repeatedly his ability to absorb knowledge. Foreign languages he absorbed like a sponge, and the classical ones had settled in his vocabulary from his early youth.

Yet the remarkable thing about the following story is that George accepted his place in a *team*. Early failures taught him the need to have friends. Today we all talk endlessly about teamwork. Assembling a team appears to be the road to success in all activities, from military matters to school projects. Your average CEO searches for an ideal team-member. There is nothing new in this. One particular application of the principle of teamwork has been in crime, and the American gang of 1872 is a landmark outfit.

Think of a successful group of crooks, neatly defined by the media as a gang. There will be the 'brains' and the 'muscle' and personnel will include a planner and a doer, with an executive at he very heart of the crew. But the notion is to be organic. Not that Jesse James or Cole Younger would have used that word. More likely their method of ensuring cohesion was a pistol to the temple and a firm threat of using a bullet as a means of executive action. Still, the thinking has always been the same: have all members gel smoothly together and make each guy's expertise a source of both pride and usefulness.

Scanning the history of crime, we can pick out gangs held together by fear, by greed, by fun, and by sheer tough necessity. The Bidwell brothers inclined to accept that a mix of greed and fun were the essentials, but their 'long firm' approach, working out a period of six months over which they would plan and carry out their daring bank robbery, has a smack of Butch Cassidy and Sundance about it – just without the guns.

In Britain when they arrived, the gangs usually preferred to agree that desperation was their motive for highway robbery or for property theft. But at the very point that the Bidwells and George arrived, London and other cities were in the grip of a very particular moral panic. Crooks seemed to be more interested in assault and murder than in bank accounts

In the early 1860s there was a virtual epidemic of a new method of assault: garrotting. Up to 17 July, 1862 there had been only fifteen robberies with violence in the city of London. But then a Member of Parliament, one Hugh Pilkington, was 'garotted' in Pall Mall. A new and terrifying crime against the person had been noted. In its chronicle of November, 1862, The *Annual Register* reported that there had been a 'garotte terrorism' in London and in the provinces that year. The word 'garotte' was beginning to strike terror into ordinary people and newspapers were selling on headlines about this new version of street robbery. The report expresses the crime in this way:

For some years past there have been occasional instances of 'garotte robberies' - a method of highway plunder, which consists in

one ruffian seizing an unsuspecting traveller by the neck and crushing in his throat, while another simultaneously rifles his pocket; the scoundrels then decamp, leaving their victim on the ground writhing in agony...

The popular magazine, *Punch*, covered the menace with its usual acuteness and dash; one cartoon shows some middle-class theatre-goers venturing out into the streets with a platoon of soldiers guarding them. It was nothing less than a reign of terror and it gradually became much more widespread than simply London's theatre land.

This 'modern peril of the streets' was first described graphically as 'putting the hug on' and it had its own jargon, the gang members having particular roles. First, the man called the *front stall*, a lookout; then the *back stall* who was going to grab the booty, and finally the *nasty man* who would move in from behind to take the victim's throat. At the time, it was seen as a variety of crime that was somehow not 'British' and journalists tried to blame it on foreigners. It was often written about in terms linked to activities by Italian mobs. But soon it was realised that this heinous crime was becoming a speciality of the new criminal underclass of the expanding towns across Victorian England.

The terror even entered the realms of popular song, with lines such as:

> 'A gentleman's walking, perchance with a crutch
> he'll suddenly stagger and totter;
> don't think that the gentleman's taken too much
> he's unluckily met a garrotter....'

The result was that detectives, like Shore, had for some time been so concerned with such crimes against persons that any sense of more intellectual, subtle crime were rather distant.

But that sighting in 1872 marked an early warning in what was to be crime on a new, global scale, something that was always going to happen in the place where the great first Industrial revolution of Europe had occurred. London was the hub of a Empire that ruled the seas and which was represented by continents all coloured pink on the maps. What could have been more perfect for a springboard into white collar crime at its most impertinent, bold and daring?

The American Gang were ready to do an unthinkable scam on the Old lady of Threadneedle Street. With hindsight, Inspector Shore must have wished, from the bottom of his heart, that he and Pinkerton had crossed the road that day, and put a few searching questions to the young Americans. But he would have felt that with a tormenting hindsight, as he followed their trial at the Old Bailey and realised that they had achieved what most villains would have deemed to be impossible.

The Bank of England had been created in the last years of the seventeenth century, and for the first thirty years it operated from premises in Mercer's Hall and then at Grocer's Hall, but the land at Threadneedle Street, at the eastern end of Cheapside and Poultry (two main thoroughfares through lawyers London), not far from Newgate, was bought in 1724 and the fine building of today was gradually built, the most impressive section designed and made between 1788 and 1833, the work of the great architect and collector, Sir John Soane.

By the 1830s, the fully completed building stood magnificently at the great junction where the Royal Exchange stands, with another road leading to Fleet Street and the other up to Cheapside where the Lord Mayor's home and court were situated, at the Guildhall. It was also, for obvious reasons, only a few hundred yards from the City of London Police headquarters at Old Jewry, just a few hundred yards from the junction, close to everything it had the task of keeping safe and secure.

As many writers have noted, the building resembles a fortress, which provides a very fitting image of its nature. But in spite of that appearance, its position was absolutely in the heart of legal and commercial London, being only a short walk to the Cannon Street railway station, on the Thames, to the south, and a similarly short walk to the west took the visitor or Londoner to either St Paul's Cathedral or to the law courts on and behind Fleet Street.

The one dominant issue for the Bank spanning the previous generation and including the period of the Bidwells' fraud was the link between paper money and the bank's reserves. One main line of thought was that the reserve should be maintained at a third in the form of gold coin or equivalent bullion, and that the reserve was controlled by the notional amount existing in the funds raised by discounting bills. It had been restrictions on lending which caused the disaster of 1866. Underlying all the uncertainty was the conviction, established since Isaac Newton's statement of the gold standard- that cash should equal a certain rate of value in the gold equivalent. But of course, if a government kept rigidly to that gold equivalent, there would be no possibility of flexible investment.

Fortunately, the virtues of credit were fully appreciated at the time when businessmen issued bills of exchange. But if we spin this differently of course, we have this situation, as expressed by John Francis, in one the first histories of the Bank of England: 'All the gambling propensities of human nature were constantly solicited into action; and crowds of individuals of every description, the credulous and the suspicious... princes, nobles, politicians, patriots, lawyers, philosophers, poets... intermingled with women of all ranks, hastened to venture some portion of their property in schemes of which scarcely anything was known but the name.' That could be an excellent description of an entrepreneurial culture.

The Bank, when Austin Bidwell walked into its Western Branch, had known a severe crisis in the recent past, and it had tightened up its administration. In 1866, there had been a panic and the Governor at the time, Henry Lancelot Holland, had consulted the economic leaders in Gladstone's government and decided on a massive extension of credit to try to put things right. In the USA, Congress passed the Contraction Act, which gave the treasury the power to recall a large proportion of the greenbacks issued under Lincoln. In 1866 there were $1.8 billion in circulation, and in the following year this shrank to $1.3. Then, by 1872, when the Bidwells left her shores, the USA was in recession.

Then, as now, a recession in America affected everyone else, across the world. Ernest Seyd of the Bank of England, went to the States to help with the work of demonetizing silver, making gold coins the sole currency. In both Britain and America, the fears were based on the consequences of inflation and economic depression. The Banks of both nations faced the problem of how to help the economy out of the misery. It has always been the same dilemma: whether to back and extend credit and so back business, and create jobs, or to hold everything in and hope that austerity achieves something like stability in the end.

Holland's decision was to expand credit. Neil Irwin, in his book, *The Alchemists,* explains what happened: '...it would have been the equivalent of the federal reserve extending about $3.5 trillion in the aftermath of the 2008 Lehman Brothers crisis.' But it worked. By 1872, as the records of the Bank of England directors shows, investment was burgeoning; the railways and the commercial fleets were borrowing and fuelling new developments in all areas of transport and administration; insurance was booming, and the massive banks such as Barings and Rothschilds were involved in a seemingly endless stream of credit applications. It was an age of invention and of bold entrepreneurs, and until the States regrouped and expanded in the last decades of the century, the British Empire found its power escalating at a giddy rate.

The Old Lady in Threadneedle Street was run by a formidable board of directors. These 24 men in 1872 constituted the movers and shakers of the commercial and cultural world in Britain and beyond. At the centre was Alfred Charles de Rothschild, born in 1842 and at thirty, actively involved in the Bank's business. He was a close friend of the Prince of Wales, and he had started work in banking when he was just 21, becoming a Director of the bank of England in 1868; he stayed there in that post until 1889.

Other Directors then were Sir Mark Collet, later Governor, and made a baronet for his work in relation to the National Debt; there was John Saunders Gilliat, Governor later on, and also a

Conservative M.P. Another very prominent Director, a man of great wealth, was Charles Frederick Huth, from a family not far behind the Rothschilds in their power and influence. Huth was, as J Mordaunt Crook quoted, 'the epitome of caution' and he 'always disapproved of excessive luxury, considering it wrong that bankers should blossom out as landed gentry.'

Henry Riversdale Grenfell was later to be Governor also, and was, in the 1880s, vie-president of the International Monetary Congress. Then there was Charles Goschen, whose family's business interests extended to the London and San Francisco Bank, the Mexican Railway Co., and the directorship of the Hudson Bay Company.

Most of the Board of Directors may be found among the wealthier families who built their mansions in the fashionable areas of west London, where the *haut ton* of society had been maintained much as it was in Jane Austen's day. One marker of their status and privilege is to check out the elite and exclusive club called Almacks, which had been established back in 1765. For instance, by the 1890s the names of Baring and Grenfell figure prominently in the members' lists, and in fact, no less than fifteen Grenfells were members by the mid 1890s.

Scottish interests were not forgotten either: on the Board sat Alexander Matheson, nephew of Sir James Matheson, a baronet and Lord Lieutenant of Ross. Alexander sat alongside Rothschild, Goschen and the rest at that meeting in summer 1872: he made huge amounts of money in India, and on his return he made a 'good marriage' into the blue blood of aristocracy, marrying a sister of Baron Beaumont. He spent unbelievably massive amounts of cash on his estates, including the building of a completely new castle at Ardross. When he died, he was in possession of a quarter of a million acres.

They were a top elite among many elites at the hub of empire, and they took the banking business very seriously. They were the kind of men who made a decision and carried it through, immediately delegating duties to people down the chain of command in their vast communication systems. But nevertheless, in that world of expanding credit, when entrepreneurs were welcomed and likely to be backed if they were the right kind of businessmen, there were always problems, practical difficulties to overcome, and most of all, there was the human factor.

The records of the meetings of this Court of Directors through the Victorian years shows what the nature of the human element was, and they make it clear that the Court had little time for niceties and delay; they helped employees when there were cases of real distress and personal tragedy, but slackness was not tolerated and staff were constantly checked and observed.

When the Court met in 1872 it had responsibility not only for HQ at Threadneedle Street, but also for fifteen branches. Its appointed agents at these branches were essential to the success of the great smooth-running machine that was the Old Lady, at the hub of British civilization.

Yet, within this great immoveable symbol of power, with its classical architecture and seemingly infinite resources, there was that human element, and the Court of Directors, not long before Austin Bidwell walked through its doors, had faced some glitches in its systems: in May, 1872 the Court was concerned with a problem in the handling of coupons. These were yet another variety of promissory note – a piece of paper stating that a payment will be made on the presentation of the coupon. The Court reported, that May, that they had enquired 'into the circumstances attending the loss of 19 coupons amounting to £102 10 shillings.' These came from loans to the Cape of Good Hope and to New Zealand. What happened was that the Bank had a sequence of actions in which coupons were processed, and it was a clumsy one. On this occasion, a part-time worker ruined the process: 'On the present occasion it appears that Mr Davis, who was appointed *pro tempore* to assist the ledger clerks' collected a parcel and took it, 'without examination' to the Bill Office.

The result was that 'the committee feel that great laxity must have existed in the system of check or this loss would have been discovered…' In other words, the great Bank was not faultless. It was a warning of what was to come, but clearly, the criminal fraternity would be constantly looking for such weaknesses, and that simple and perfunctory note presages the kind of frauds that were to come.

As to the Western Branch in wealthy Mayfair, it figures in the Court's records usually in this brief statement, reported at virtually every meeting:

'A report from Mr Brook was read, stating that he had taken an audit of customers' securities at the Western Branch, comprised In the section marked '7,' and had found the same in the safe custody of the agent.'

The Branch always figured in that simple, matter-of-fact way – until the American gang came, like a fox to the chicken-house.

What was this Western Branch to which Austin Bidwell came to initiate his criminal plans, and who was the man in charge, the man on whom all the gang's designs and preparatory work depended for success? Bidwell, in the persona of Mr Warren, entrepreneur, walked into the Branch with the air of a man who knew his own importance, and who had presence. He fully expected that the Bank's man in charge would be equally assured and confident. After all, Britain had a global reputation for being beyond comparison in the professionalism of the men who generated and sustained their invisible exports, and it was invisible exports, such as Lloyd's marine insurance and the flotation of railway companies, which was expanding the Empire and turning the world map red.

Branches were opened, from the late 1820s onwards, largely to increase the bank's control of paper money; before that date, smaller provincial banks had printed their own notes, and gradually the government had marginalised these by Acts which restricted their expansion; then along came the Bank Charter Act of 1844 which stopped all new banks from issuing notes, and any bank which had more than six partners could not issue paper money either. The result was that Threadneedle Street was the absolute heart of money circulation, along with other methods of transactions such as post bills, bills of exchange and cheques.

The Bank of England opened the Western Branch on 1 October, 1855, to work as an ordinary banking house, that is, with practically no accounts relating to the government. There was to be close co-operation of course, between the Old Lady herself in Threadneedle Street, and the Western Branch. The latter was situated within the magnificent Uxbridge House in Mayfair. Uxbridge House had been built for Lord Uxbridge in the 1790s, situated around the corner from Bond Street and the Burlington Arcade, both still some of today's most grand and stylish shopping places in London.

As soon as the Bank of England had been established, back in 1694, the creation of branches was suggested; but things moved very slowly, and it was not until 1826 that the first provincial branches were opened in three towns: Gloucester, Manchester and Swansea. In London itself, there was no branch until the Western one, the only other city bank being the later 1881 branch dealing with the Supreme Court.

In 1855 there was no excitement at the opening of the new branch. *The Times* simply devoted one sentence to it, announcing that the branch had opened 'under the management of Mr C. Tindal.' But it was a magnificent location for the kind of large-scale commercial transactions it was destined to deal with. A wide stone Doric portico had been built in the 1850s, and then the old dining room was converted into the main office. There was also a large and stylish committee room, and in the upper parts, as one report noted, 'will be appropriated to the residences of Captain Tindal R.N., the manager, and Mr Miller, the sub-manager.' The other main conversions from Lord Uxbridge's huge residence involved, as one writer noted, the creation of a 'south-west ante-room... united with the truncated great drawing-room to form a large office with two compartments. In other words, the Western Branch comprised two vast floors of the opulent Georgian building, which was celebrated in an 1855 feature on the opening in the *Illustrated London News*, a typical exercise in relishing yet another part of the great foundation in the city which was in the hub of the British Empire.

Into this impressive new extension of the Old lady came Colonel Peregrine Francis. His arrival was noted in the Bank's journal records for 23 May, 1872:

'It was recommended to the Court of Directors that Colonel Peregrine Madgwick Francis, Agent at the Hull branch, be appointed agent at the Western Branch with a salary of £1,500 a year on the retirement of Mr Robert Ruthven Lyon...'

That was indeed a handsome salary: in present day values his £1,500 would be around £60,000. Such a man would be exemplary; he would carry massive responsibility and he would have to have that essential quality of style and moral probity which had at that time to stand out, prominent as his classy suit and impeccable manner.

Francis was born on 1 July, 1818, baptized at St Leonard's in Shoreditch, London, the church immortalised in the rhyme 'when I grow rich/say the bells of Shoreditch,' so he knew London in his childhood and in his formative years. His father was a merchant, and was a wealthy man, his home being in Brunswick Place, Marylebone, not far from Regent's Park.

He had started his career in banking, up in East Yorkshire, after his army career. Francis had been an officer in the army of the East India Company, which had been the major factor in controlling India and regulating all Britain's commercial interests since the opening of the seventeenth century. He had been trained at the military training school at Addiscombe in Surrey, in 1833-34, afterwards going out to India, where he married Emma Thomas in Madras on August 22, 1849. When the Company ceased its control and handed over responsibilities to the Army of India in 1861, he retired and came back to Britain.

He was based in the city of Hull when recruited for London, on the Humber estuary, the great fishing port, with its mass of trawlers and freighters. It was a port facing towards Europe: the masses of people escaping the religious persecution in Eastern Europe passed through Hull, many on their way across northern England to Liverpool, where they could board a ship bound for New York and their new lives as Americans.

There were all kinds of reshufflings of staff across the branches at the time. Just a few weeks after Francis started, Captain Percy Lempriere, who had been sub-agent with Francis at Hull, was moved to Leeds. He had had the misfortune to lose two of his children to the common killer diseases of the time, typhus and TB. The Bank took a close interest in its employees and was generally humane and considerate in its attitudes to their domestic circumstances. After the relocation of staff, Colonel Peregrine Francis, by 1872 the father of six children (so he would need that large salary) was obviously someone who impressed his superiors at Head Office in London.

Colonel Francis and Captain Lempriere were, of course, military men. It was the policy at that time to place ex-officers in a number of important professional positions: they manned the prisons, led the police force and found new careers in all varieties of public administration. At Northallerton prison in the north of England, for instance, the Governor had been one of the famous officers of the 'six hundred' in the Charge of the Light Brigade in the battle of Balaclava in 1854, during the Crimean War.

It was the policy of the Bank to employ as their branch agents men who had two essential qualities: local knowledge and sound business knowledge. The latter quality comprised both fiscal knowledge and a strong ethical fabric in their character. Being an employee of the Old Lady meant having moral rectitude and the right kind of behaviour at all times. The records of the Court of Directors show a continual monitoring of any staff, from clerks to senior managers, who might be falling short of the mark. Colonel Francis, although he had been based in Hull, had the right moral sense, being an army man, and he knew London. It would have been hard to find an army officer at the time who did not know London. As memoirs of senior officers often show, the general trajectory of the training arc they had was one in which acquaintance with London clubs and theatres was *de rigueur*.

Francis, by the time of Bidwell's arrival, had been running the branch for only four months, but he was every inch the sophisticated, cultured type required by that responsible post: he was articulate, charming yet precise; he was a good listener, and he clearly had the ability of close observation and knowledge of the world so essential in transactions involving large sums of money. He had seen service in India earlier in life, and was a practical man as well as a man of affairs.

But there was more to the Bank of England's work than paper money or loans; they were operating at a time when trade was expanding beyond all comprehension, and it was international. By the middle of the nineteenth century, the nature of credit across the business empires was absolutely massive. On the domestic front, the expanding railway companies borrowed huge amounts-sometimes, as in 1872, £7,000 – a sum in modern terms close on £600,000.

In mid-1872, just as Peregrine Francis was settling in at his new desk, and no doubt taking in the wonderful grandeur of his daily surroundings, which contrasted sharply with his much smaller and more workaday Hull office, there was action being taken to control and regulate the discounting of bills of exchange. These documents and transactions were at the very hub of the commercial world around the Bank. These bills are defined in the legislation as 'An unconditional order in writing addressed by one person to another, signed by the person giving it, requesting the person to whom it is addressed to pay at some fixed or determinable future time a fixed sum in money to or to the order of a specified person or bearer.' In other words, it operated like a cheque, but it normally had a defined period in which it had to be used, and the point is that it allowed time for the issuing person to gather cash or assets, or alternatively, it confirmed his credit standing with the bank concerned.

The bill of exchange therefore committed the bank to part with the sums of money accrued as the bills were taken at the cashiers' counters. Why did the banks do all this? The answer is quite simply, profit. They charged a discount- a fee – for the transaction, and it was the source of considerable profit. During the middle months of 1872, when Francis was the new man at the Western Branch, the Court of Directors minuted a sequence of reductions in the percentages of discounts on such bills. In early May, the records noted: ' Amended... that the minimum rate of discount on bills not having more than 95 days to run be raised from 4 to 5 per cent.' A bill of one thousand pounds would earn them £50- a large sum in the 1870s. That was for a bill with a short time in which cash had to be paid on it. But later that year, for bills with 95 days to run (which the Bank preferred of course) the discount rate was lowered in stages down to 3%. But a bill with less than 95 days had the rate increased to 6% by July of 1872.

All this meant that, as Colonel Francis was meeting and interviewing customers, the directors at headquarters were working out profits; yet they were doing much more. They were aware that bills of exchange needed to be carefully supervised and checked. There was always a threat. That vulnerability to fraud may be seen in the accounts presented to the Court from their solicitors, Freshfields, which is today an international law firm with 2,400 lawyers around the globe. When they presented their bills for services rendered in August, 1872, it included this item:

'Charges in connection with the measures taken to detect and punish forgeries Upon the Bank………………£14.13.2

In fact, the cost to the Bank for legal services in the short period of six months in that year was over £380. Peace of mind is expensive, as the value of that sum today is around £30,000.

In 1872, then, the great bank at the centre of the British Empire was full of confidence, enjoying almost a complete monopoly of credit in the larger, most prominent area of the world markets it dealt with, and its Board of Directors, through their regular court meetings, checked and regulated everything that happened, almost down to the last paper-clip in the smallest office. Yet beneath this apparent assurance and self-esteem, there was that worm in the apple, the possibility of there being a criminal smart enough to exploit its systems and protocols.

The rest is history. There was a massive fraud on the bank. The gang were caught because they were greedy, and used one last forged document. Even in court, MacDonnell amused his overactive brain by translating the proceedings into Greek.

*

Turnkeys and Warders
Researching the lives and social history of prison staff in Georgian and Victorian Britain

Early History
The first prison staff were keepers, employed by the local sheriff or Lord of the Manor. For many centuries, there was never even the faintest discussion of those looking after prisoners being conceived as professionals, with any kind of controls and qualifications.

Medieval prisons as custodial places – temporary places for people awaiting trial – are linked mainly to the status of the sheriff, as he was responsible for bringing an alleged criminal to trial. After the Assize of Clarendon in 1166, periods of gaol confinement become more common. Many prisoners were detained for committing a felony, for treason or for forest offences. In addition, debtors began to be detained by the marshall until a trial concluded. In the thirteenth and fourteenth centuries sheriffs, marshalls and others committed people to the Fleet or Tower prisons in London. Most prisoners did not, as famous people did in the Tower, dine with the constable and have a comfortable bed. Most gaols were sheriffs' prisons, and the stories of prisons across the land, together with the dozens of London gaols established since Newgate (from 1423) and the Marshalsea (eleventh century) are mostly of common people.

At York there were always problems with the gaolers being bribed and helping prisoners escape. The gaolers were also fond of extracting money from prisoners, it seems. In 1388 a commission was formed to bring to justice the Yorker gaoler, William Holgate, issued by the sheriff of Yorkshire, John Saville. Holgate was accused of 'Permitting divers felons therein to escape, and compelled other prisoners by duress and divers penalties to become approvers (informers) and to appeal lieges of the King of felony, whom he caused to be taken and detained in the said gaol, he extorting sums of money from them and withdrawing the alms given for their maintenance.' He soon joined his charges behind bars.

The root of so much abuse was that gaolers in local gaols rarely had a fee. From the earliest local gaols there had been sporadic fees paid in some prisons, but there was no national or regional system of fees. The gaoler or turnkey had to exist by taking a number of fees from their prisoners. This was known as 'garnish' in the argot of the time, and everyone suffered, perhaps most of all the debtors, as one writer explains in a letter to the *Gentleman's Magazine*: '*If gaolers do not have large salaries for the execution of their office, let the public pay them and let not the sufferings of the wretched be increased by their rapine... My companions here are debtors, who though they have either satisfied or been forgiven by their creditors cannot obtain their liberty till Mr Gaoler is paid his fees. Here therefore they languish, many of them with cold and hunger and some with infirmity and disease till death sets them free without fee or reward.'*

The gaols were limbos of neglect, with a range of punishments in the tough regimes maintained by the tyrants who held the keys and the food supplies. A few humanitarians occasionally tried to change things, but one additional problem was that offices and responsibilities of all kinds were up for sale, in an age of nepotism and corruption. The Georgian period and Regency were times in which sinecures were bought and sold as a matter of everyday business. A publication called *The Red Book* listed these offices and their value. A typical example was the Wardenship of the Cinque Ports, which paid a thousand pounds a year. A celebrated case was that of Ashley Cowper, younger brother of William Cowper, who was a barrister in 1723. He was also a Mason and a member of the Horn Lodge; Ashley acquired the post of Clerk to the Parliaments, a very well-paid and esteemed post. The post was in fact bought for him by his father, who just happened to be Judge Spence Cowper.

There was no investigation into nepotism and sinecures until 1780. The situation was, as Blake Pinnell has explained, that 'The law courts, the established church, part of the army and the royal household contained many positions in which the occupants did very little for the money they received.

Horrors and Abuse at the Fleet

In the management of prisons, this was a very dangerous and destructive practice, particularly as the man who bought the governorship could stay away from the prison as often as he liked, and leave a minion in charge. One of the very worst of these abuses was highlighted in the case of John Huggins, warden of the Fleet prison, who was tried at the Old Bailey in 1729 for the murder of one of his charges, Edward Arne.

Huggins bought the wardenship of the Fleet for the huge sum of £5,000 for himself and his son. Of course he then had to get the investment back, by any means possible. The Fleet was at that time mainly a debtors' prison, and we know what it was like because the great reformer John Howard reported on it. At that time, debtors' prisons had two sides: Common and the Masters. On the latter side lived those who could afford to rent their accommodation, but the Common side, as Howard describes, was horrendous:

'The apartments for the Common-side debtors are only part of the right wing... Besides the cellar there are four floors. On each floor is a room about twenty four or five feet square, with a fire-place; and on the sides seven closets or cabins to sleep in. Such of the prisoners who swear in court or before a commissioner that they cannot subsist without charity, have the donations which are sent to the prison, and the begging box and grate.'

The grate was the street level aperture from which they could beg passers-by for alms or even just water. But their situation would have normally been like that of the anonymous writer to the *Gentleman's Magazine*, were it not for the fact that John Huggins and his gang of assistants were sadists. At the basis of the sentence was the table of fees for the gaolers: these included fees for the chaplain, the porter, the chamberlain, the turnkey, and added to that were fees for 'liberty of the house and irons when first coming in' and a dismission fee. The total cost of all these fees was supposed to be under £2.0s.0d. but in fact £3.5s.0d. was the sum taken, as increments were applied.

Huggins decided, as he aged, that he would sell his position to a certain Thomas Bambridge, his deputy, along with another scoundrel called Dougal Cuthbert. A barbaric and murderous regime was to follow, and the scandal broke not long after Bambridge took over control. At the centre of the affair was the death of a prisoner, Edward Arne, who had been committed to a horrible den called the Strong Room where he starved and was submitted to infections and diseases so extreme that he lost his wits before dying a miserable death inside the walls.

At the trial, the Strong room was described by a witness called Bigrave:

Solicitor-General: What do you know of the building the strong room?

Bigrave: When I came there I saw there was a stable which was converted into a strong room . . .

Solicitor-General: What sort of a place is it?

Bigrave: It is arched like a wine vault, built of brick and mortar.

'Locals'

There were still abuses and scandals in the nineteenth century, as a string of notorious cases makes clear, from the failure of the Millbank penitentiary to cases of cruelty in the mid-century at Birmingham and Leicester. Millbank was built between 1813 and 1816, with three miles of corridors. Thirty years later, it had been downgraded to what was basically a removal local prison, its inmates staying a short time before dispersal to other London prisons. Between four and five thousand inmates were kept there annually, but in 1870 it was used as a military prison, and then closed twenty years later.

But the local gaols were often family concerns. The houses of correction or bridewells, had been in existence since the 1550's and their residents were a mix of debtors and criminals, and they were conceived as houses of industry, out to make a profit, so the families had that mindset when they staffed the places.

In the early years of the nineteenth century, when houses of correction had become widely established, the Shepherd family ran Northallerton house of correction. The matron was the governor's wife, and their son was employed as 'keeper of silence.'

In 1837 he wrote to his friend in York, and this letter gives us a clear picture of the problems in maintaining vigilance and control- just as difficult then as now:

'Dear George,

I have received your letter. Your apprenticeship with your uncle in York is no doubt of great interest. You seem displeased with your lot against mine. To answer you, yes, my father is Keeper of the prison and mother is the Matron. They did give me the post at £50 a year, but George, this is a House of Correction, where Inspectors visit regularly. One has just made his visit and he said I was very youthful for such a position [he was aged seventeen] which requires great moderation and command of temper. He also added and put down in his report, during the course of his inspection he had no reason to believe the post to be inadequately filled. The parson caused quite a to do just before the Inspector arrived. He likes to distribute tracts and books to the untried prisoners. The Inspector looked through them and found a piece on secret writing and invisible ink. When he visited our hospital he found some of our prisoners experimenting with it . . . It's not easy this job, George, the prisoners are wily as foxes. If any infringe the rules, I take them before the Keeper. I took one boy yesterday for turning his head to the side while reading. He answered he was obliged to do so as it was so dark in the mess room. Father believed him and let him go unpunished. He said it was no offence. I wasn't best pleased, I'm sure he was preparing to whisper to a friend. Next time, I'll wait until he does so, then I'll have him in solitary. He won't dupe me . . .'

This was William Shepherd, and he was clearly the right material for prison work; he was governor by 1849, as he is listed in that position in *Slater's Directory of Yorkshire and Lincolnshire*. He followed his father, Thomas, in that capacity.

The staff were generally well paid; in the first decades of the prison's existence the keeper was paid from £160-£200 and a fee of a few shillings was paid to him for each discharged prisoner. He also had a range of 'perks' paid to him until the 1840s when he received a salary: this followed a recommendation by the inspector in which he wrote: 'I most strongly recommend that that the whole of the keeper's perquisites should be abolished and a fixed stipend paid him.' Turnkeys were usually retired police constables and by 1837 their pay was £50. As for the assistant to the turnkey, he could be something of an odd-job man; one of these was a barber and clerk doing chapel work in addition to the work of a warden. The rest of the supervisory staff were the young keeper of silence and a watchman.

We know something of the staff lives and women prisoners at the large London prisons through memoirs. In 1862 'A prison matron' published *Female Life in Prison* for instance, and there she wrote that in the system there were 'four principal matrons, one chief matron, whose supervision is less confined to the prisoners than to their subordinate officers, and there are also supernumeraries who are engaged on "flying missions" to whom is not entrusted the charge of a ward.' She mentions a total of 36 female officers at Brixton, and at the huge Millbank, she notes that, ' In case of an outbreak... the female officers have the warders of the men's prison within call.'

Nationalised and Rationalised
It is something of a paradox that it was Disraeli's Conservatives who passed the 1877 Prisons Act and brought about centralisation. Such policies were not entrenched in their manifesto, but it was an age of pragmatism in politics and all the sensible arguments were applied in the debate. It was the Home Secretary, Asheton Cross, who introduced the bill for its first reading. His main contentions were that the prisons were expensive to manage and that the system was outdated, with too many small prisons on the list in the provinces. Behind the move was a basic political fact: the Conservatives had promised to reduce local rates and taking the prisons into centralisation was one way to do that.

Cross made an influential speech, with issues of waste and poor management along with a critique of the state of the prisons. There were opponents, of course; the main argument against was the same one that had been applied when other services were centralised – factories, education and so on. The voices against the move said that there would be incompetence, huge rises in running costs and that it was just not right to interfere with the principal of local government.

But the thought that at last a great deal of power would be taken from local magistrates pleased many; they were totally autonomous, and so that power was always going to be open to abuse. The Act would place the Home Secretary in control and naturally, he was a part of the functioning of parliament. There were objections from the provinces: a petition from Nottingham was presented, and Oxford City Council complained, stating that they had only recently spent a very large sum of money on their establishment, and if it were to change then that would have been wasted. But after a debate on 12th July, the bill became law.

The Secretary of State was now the person in command of the prison service. It was he who would appoint staff and he would have the powers previously in the hands of the justices, those powers applied to acts, common law and to charters. Justices in their normal work were no longer to have any direct influence on prisons; visiting justices were to be in place, something that prefigured the later boards of visitors.

The new organisation at the centre was the Prison Commission, with five Commissioners. The new body would have to make reports to parliament and appoint the senior staff across the country. The first Commissioner was, of course, Sir Edmund Du Cane. It has been said about the man that he could boast that he could look at his watch at any time of the day and know exactly what any one of the prisoners in England would be doing. Du Cane was a product of the

Royal Military Academy at Woolwich; he became a lieutenant in the Royal Engineers when he was only eighteen, and retired with the rank of major-general in 1887. He had worked in convict prisons in Western Australia, and his interest in the prison system grew partly through his friendship with Sir Edward Henderson, Chief Commissioner of the Metropolitan Police. In 1863 he was appointed as Director of Convict prisons and Inspector of Military Prisons. He was knighted in 1877 when he took the job as Commissioner in the new prison system.

Du Cane held the belief that a criminal tendency is the basis of all mankind, and saw 'career criminals' as fools who were too weak ever to look into themselves and change; hence he rejected the religion-based attitudes of previous years. The task ahead in 1877 was to make prisons cost-effective and places so formidable that they would be a deterrent. He came up with a four-stage regime for the prisoner:

Stage 1 (nine months) held in absolute separation, and with 6-10 hours of hard labour each day. He had no mattress for the first two weeks of the sentence and was allowed only religious books.
Stage 2 The work became less severe; he was allowed limited association and one library book per week.
Stage 3 A small release gratuity was in place and more books available
Stage 4 He was now eligible for special employment and the release gratuity was raised.

As with all cost-cutting enterprises, places and people were dispensed with across the land: by the time of Du Cane's retirement in 1895, the number of local prisons had been reduced from 113 to 59. Yet within the new prisons and the reformed ones, the tough regimes went on, with a reinforcement of the hard labour when *penal servitude* was conceived and implemented in 1853 as an alternative to transportation. This referred to a graded trajectory of prison work within the current regime, based on work and discipline. The Prison Act of 1865 had implemented a harsh prison regime based on 'hard labour, hard board and hard fare' and the 'hard labour element in this meant long hours of pointless sweat-work such as cutting stones, labouring or 'work which visibly quickens the breath and opens the pores.' A major part of this was the treadmill or tread wheel, which was invented by William Cubitt in 1819 after he had seen prisoners at Bury St Edmunds, as he put it, 'lounging about.' This was a giant wheel powered by human leg-power as prisoners stepped up onto platforms simply to turn the wheel.

Whereas previously there had been keepers, a matron, turnkeys and gate-keepers, from the mid-Victorian years there was a gradual move to regulate staff, and Du Cane's reforms, with the trimming-down of the prison service estate, meant that staff became unified and a hierarchy properly imposed. But even earlier than 1877, there had been a system of 'inferior' and 'superior' officers. The parliamentary enquiries of that period show listings with special duties and responsibilities, but a typical situation was that warders received emoluments for dealing with rations and medical attendance, while other staff such as gardeners, carpenters and clerks of works had no allowances.

Superior officers included a range of clerical posts, religious and medical people and messengers. The report from Millbank in 1846 lists such specific posts as 'Secretary and accountant' and 'Transport clerk' for instance. At that time, there was transportation in progress (until the 1860s) and Mr Flockhart and Mr Stewart, religious instructors, were 'appointed to instruct prisoners on their voyage to the penal colonies.'

In 1881 at Lincoln prison, categories of staff were typical of the new situation: there were matron, clerk, warder, assistant warder, night watchman and gatekeeper. Often, the other ancillary staff were part-time. But the specialists such as chaplain, doctor and other support staff were a mix of real specialists and local professionals.

Between c.1850 and 1900, then, prison staff had become part of a streamlined, efficient hierarchy in a range of prisons, from local to large convict establishments. There were the beginnings of a rigid and regulated career structure for staff, but still there were problems, mainly due to the military-style order and supervision of prisoners in the radial prisons with their central observation towers. But at least there was education and more productive work. The dreaded treadmill disappeared in the 1890s though the crank was still used - a machine fixed to the wall outside a cell, and leading to a handle inside which had to be turned so many times each day, subject to punishment.

Yet for the staff, by the end of Victoria's reign there was surely a feeling that the prisons, run like the army, were at least certain in their 'targets' and in the force of their regime, as they reflected the morals and values of the great empire that Britain had become by the end of the century.

Where to research the Lives of Prison Staff

- In parliamentary papers: reports and enquiries throughout the nineteenth century often contain names of staff and dialogues featuring them during interviews by commissioners.
- In directories and yearbooks etc. For instance, Kelly's Directory will list main staff under 'Her/His Majesty's prison, and these will include Governor, Chaplain, Medical Officer, Steward, Chief Officer and Matron.
- In the local press. Local and regional newspapers often have reports on prisoners' aid societies such as groups working to arrange rehabilitation or to help with severe financial problems of ex-offenders.
- In materials at archives offices, in county records etc.

Select Bibliography

Anon. *Female Life in Prison* (Hurst and Blackett, 1862)
Norval Morris and David J Rothman, *The Oxford History of the Prison* (OUP., 1998)
Philip Priestley, *Victorian Prison Lives* (Pimlico, 1999)
Anthony Stokes, *Pit of Shame: The Real Ballad of Reading Gaol* Waterside Press, 2007)
J E Thomas, *The English Prison Officer Since 1850* (Routledge and Kegan Paul, 1972)

**

6

Irish Themes

The Dublin Castle Story and Irish Police Records

In 1885, Joseph Chamberlain said, 'I say the time has come to reform altogether the absurd and irritating anachronism which is known as Dublin Castle.' The fact that he saw it as a problem indicates its power and status. In effect, that wish was not fulfilled until the Castle was handed over to the new Provisional Government in January 1922.

As a recent edition of the guide to Dublin Castle proclaimed, the place is at the heart of Irish history 'Tourists and commuters walk past the gates every day, and the towers are on the skyline, but few know the profound material establishment inside those walls, with underground level foundations and the now subterranean river Poddle, which ran alongside the Liffey in the centuries when the Vikings controlled what was to become Dublin'.

The Castle has been the scene of bold escapes and cruel detentions, sieges and important decisions; government and military strategy, and indeed, during the 1916 Easter Rising, one of the key sites held when the Republicans took on the British garrison. Whatever stance is taken to assess the stronghold within the city, the fact that is has been the centre of colonial rule is inescapable:

people detained for political reasons were held and questioned there and military intelligence had its base inside the high walls.

The Castle has been there since 1204, when King John ordered its construction, and from that time it was, in many people's opinion, maintained as an establishment entirely on its own: an institution reminding everyone who stopped to reflect on it, that it existed as a court in miniature, with the Lord Lieutenant of Ireland existing in a vice-regal capacity.

In 1893 a magazine called *The Idler* had a feature on the Lord Lieutenant in a series called 'Lions in their Dens' which had the attitude of indulging in celebrity worship. The author, Raymond Blathwayt, was conducted around the halls and towers by the Lord Lieutenant's sister, Mrs Arthur Henniker, and we may gain a picture of what life was like at the time with Blathwayt's account of walking in with her:

'. . . we passed two sentries on guard at the entrance to the great hall, and proceeded up a staircase lined with rifles and through long, sunlit corridors, "You must come with me to my own special sanctum . . ." Here, in a lofty, white-panelled room, with windows looking down upon the private gardens of the castle in which His Excellency and one of the ADC's were walking up and down, Mrs Henniker and I sat talking about the past . . .'

The feature contains line drawings of guests arriving in carriages, elegant couples walking up the grand staircase to a ball, masses of guests waiting to be 'presented' to His Excellency and a solemn photograph of ADC' in a group, some with bearskin hats, and others sporting kilts, plumes in hats and a multitude of braids, ribbons and medals. Outside, in the slums of the city, there were thousands living in tenements, hospitals full of paupers and disease rife among the poor, creating an alarmingly high infant mortality rate.

In its more recent history, the Castle has been the focus for one of the strangest mysteries in modern Irish history. On the morning of Saturday 6 July, 1907, a cleaning lady called Mary Farrell, working at Dublin Castle, was going about her duties and had reached the library when she noticed that the door was unlocked. She had found the same situation three days before that but no action had been taken by Sir Arthur Vicars when it was reported. Vicars was the Ulster King of Arms and he was responsible not merely for the security of the library and rooms around, but for something far more important – the Insignia of the Most Illustrious order of St Patrick, otherwise known as the Irish 'Crown Jewels.'

These were in a safe in the library because when the safe had been taken to the Castle from a bank vault, in order to be kept at the Office of Arms, it was found that the safe was too large to be taken in, so it was placed in the library of the Bedford Tower. Not only was it a solid safe, it was also in a position where soldiers and police officers would always be in close proximity, so it must have seemed a safe place to store such valuables. How wrong could the men responsible have been – because later on after the cleaner made the second report on the sixth of the month, William Stivey, who was an assistant to Vicars, went to the safe and found that it was unlocked and that the jewels had gone.

The jewels were the insignia of a group formed by George III in 1783, as an Irish form of the famous Scottish order of the Thistle. The jewels had been made in London by a company called Rundell and Bridge and the glory of the collection comprised two items: a star and badge of the Order of St Patrick. The statutes and rules of the order had only recently been revised – just two years previously – and the Office of Arms had been moved to the Castle in that year. There was a whole panoply of officers and honorary members entrusted with the safety of the jewels, including the Dublin Herald Frank Shackleton, who was the brother of the famous explorer. He became a suspect, because clearly the valuables had been stolen by someone with access to a key, and he lodged with Vicars at his home in Clonskeagh Road.

Sir Arthur Vicars was born in Leamington in 1864, the son of Sir Arthur Edward Vicars, Colonel in the 61st Regiment. He had been educated at Magdalen College, Oxford, and then in 1893 he was appointed as Ulster King of Arms. *The Times* wrote of him on his death, 'He was thoroughly versed in the sciences of heraldry and genealogy… He was a Fellow of the Royal Society of Antiquaries and a trustee of the National Library of Ireland.' Vicars had actually been the man who founded the Heraldic Museum at the Office of Arms. But all this counted for nothing after the disgrace and scandal of this daring and outrageous theft.

Vicars had in his possession the only two keys to the safe. One of the first lines of thought was that Shackleton had used or copied one of these. They had not actually been seen since 11 June, when Vicars had proudly shown them to a visitor, the librarian of the Duke of Northumberland. It was rare for anyone to open the safe but Vicars himself, and so for him to ask Stivey to open it, and to give him a key, on the day the theft was discovered, was a notable fact when the investigation began.

The police suspected Shackleton but on slender information, including the detail that a few days before the theft he had been heard to remark that one day the jewels might well be stolen. He was also in debt, and so had a motive.

It was a major scandal: the status of the Office of Arms was of the highest order; they had been established in 1552, and they administered the protocol and precedence at Dublin Castle. Vicars, as Ulster Kings of Arms was the Chief Herald of Ireland, Knight Attendant and registrar of the Order. In the records he was defined as ' the first and only permanent officer of the Lord Lieutenant's household.' A painting of Sir Arthur Vicars in his ceremonial dress is at the Castle, showing him in Elizabethan court garb, with doublet and ruff, and with the harp of Ireland prominent on the lower left side of his garments.

The police went into action. They issued a poster offering one thousand pounds reward for information leading to the retrieval of the jewels. They are described there as having 150 white, pure diamonds issuing from the centre' and the badge was 'set in silver, with a shamrock of emeralds on a ruby cross surrounded by a sky blue enamelled circle – with their motto, *Quis superabit* (who shall separate it). The whole was 'surrounded by a circle of large single Brazilian stones, surmounted by a crowned harp in diamonds.'

There was to be a royal visit just four days after this discovery and that had, of course, been planned. There was to have been an investiture of a knight in St Patrick's Hall in the events of that visit, and of course that was something that caused a furore in London. The King, Edward VII, demanded that Vicars be sacked. There was a smear campaign against him, including accounts of orgies he was supposedly involved in, and the allegation that he was homosexual, which was then a criminal activity of course, and Oscar Wilde's trial was fresh in the public memory.

When it came to the establishment of a Viceregal Commission of Enquiry, after a period when there had been no success in the hunt for the villains, Vicars kept out of it. The Commission met in January, 1908 and heard evidence from Shackleton. The due process of enquiry took place and in the end Vicars was totally at fault. It vindicated Shackleton and made it clear that Vicars was a disgrace to the office. The Commission was appointed by the Irish government and included Chester Jones, a London police magistrate and the Chief Commissioner of the Dublin Metropolitan Police. At the time, it was reported by the chairman that

'Sir Arthur Vicars had definitely declined to come forward to facilitate the Commission in any way. He recognised that the Commission had no power to control or to compel Sir Arthur Vicars to give evidence. The government considered that the enquiry should go forward . . .'

Vicars was dismissed and went to live in County Kerry, where, on 14 April, 1921, a party of IRA men shot him dead. *The Times* reported on his death that he had faced a mob of gunmen before, a year earlier, and had stood firm when they demanded the key to his strong room. On that occasion they had left, but the second attack was more desperate and determined. He was taken from his bed in his dressing gown and murdered outside his house. A label was placed around his neck with the words, *'Spy, Informers beware. I.R.A. never forgets.'* His house was then set on fire.

The Garda Siochana

The Garda Siochana, formerly known as the Civic Guard, was formed in 1922 by the Irish Provisional government, to be the police constabulary of the Irish Free State. Previously there had been the Royal Irish Constabulary together with the short-lived Irish Republican Police of 1919-1922. By the Garda Siochana Act of 1923 that name was formally adopted, but the Dublin Metropolitan Police still existed until 1925 when the two forces were combined. Since that time, the Garda has been the only national police force of the Republic of Ireland, and an officer is referred to as a 'Garda' in much the same way as an English officer is called 'constable.'

The force expanded in the early 1920s; in 1923 an advertisement announced 30 vacancies for cadetships, and these were open to officers of the national army who had at least two years of experience in the Volunteers in the pre-truce years. The usual police regulations on behaviour were then sorted out, as they had been by every constabulary since Peel's 1829 Act, as in Order number 14 for instance: 'No man of any rank who is addicted to drink will be permitted to remain a member of the Civic Guard. This is a penalty which will be rigidly enforced.'

Proposals for the merger of the Garda and the Dublin Metropolitan Police were discussed in November, 1924, and the amalgamation followed the next year. A few years later we have what may be read as the mission statement of the Garda, expressed in a speech by Kevin O'Higgins: 'The internal politics and political controversies of the country are not your concern. You will serve with the same imperturbable discipline and with increasing efficiency any government which has the support of the majority...'

Today the Garda Museum is housed in Dublin Castle, containing a large collection of artefacts and memorabilia, going back to the earlier police forces, such as the one formed by Sir Robert Peel while he was Chief Secretary based in the Castle in the Regency years 1812-1818.

The Dublin Metropolitan Police
The force was formed in 1836 and existing until its amalgamation with the Garda Siochana in 1925; at the beginning, the creation of the new constabulary sprang from Sir Robert Peel's Peace Preservation Force, which he established while he was Chief Secretary for Ireland, and of course, a little later, he was responsible for the 1829 Police Act which led to the Metropolitan Police. In fact, the London force provided a template for the organisation of the new Dublin force, not only in terms of the uniform design, but also their structure was similar, with a Commissioner at the head.

In the early twentieth century, the political division – G Division – were involved in the War of Independence, including involvement with the efficient intelligence corps formed by Michael Collins. One way to glean the more dramatic elements of their history is to look at the roll of honour (see:
www.policememorial.org.uk/Forces/IRELAND/DMP_Roll.htm)

Some of these heroic characters took on extremely dangerous characters with courage and determination, such as Constable Joseph Daly, who was killed after an attack with a cleaver while arresting a man in 1881, and Inspector John Mills, who was beaten to death while escorting prisoners he had arrested at a political meeting.

In searching for ancestors in service records for this constabulary, the best place to begin is with Jim Herlihy's comprehensive reference work, *The Dublin Metropolitan Police: A Complete Alphabetical List of Officers and Men 1836-1925*, published by Four Courts Press, 2001. After that, consult the National Archives and Garda Archives, Phoenix Park, for service records, and details are at www.irishtimes.com. Another useful place to go and ask specific questions for information on police ancestors in Ireland is at Ancestry.com message boards for 'Dublin Metropolitan Police service records.'

The Royal Irish Constabulary

The force began as the Irish Constabulary, and then in 1867 the name Royal Irish Constabulary was made official. Before that, the origins were in the Irish (Constabulary, Ireland) Act of 1836. Its men had a turbulent time and won great respect, as a certain 'Resident of County Clare' wrote to *The Times* in 1878: 'I take it for granted that if the Irish people did not enlist as soldiers, they would not enlist in the Irish Constabulary, called by Her Majesty the "Royal" Irish Constabulary from the gallant stand which the members of that force made against the Fenians in 1867.'

The Constabulary was very much in the headlines during the Land Wars of the 1880s and in a letter to the press in 1881, one correspondent wrote of them: 'My object in writing is to draw the attention of the government and the country to the noble part played by a small but gallant band in Ireland... the Royal Irish Constabulary... Their bravery has been so conspicuous that on very many occasions a half-dozen men have kept in check enraged and desperate mobs of some hundreds...'

There were certainly some most remarkable men in their ranks, such as W V Harrel, who was born in 1866. At the age of twenty he joined the RIC, and by 1898 he had risen to be an inspector of prisons in Ireland. Four years later he was appointed Assistant Commissioner of the Dublin Metropolitan Police, and was honoured with a Companion of the Bath award in 1912.

The first phase of its history related solely to peace-keeping, but later it assumed revenue duties, and the force was in existence until 1922. Service records later passed to the Home Office and then they were lodged at The National Archives.

The service records are found at HO 184 arranged by service number, and with an alphabetical index; other registers list indexes for officers and for auxiliary force members. These registers have a great deal of information, covering physical features, date of appointment, length of service, place where they served and date of retirement or death. There are also pension records here, covering registers and allowances for the years 1873-1922, at reference PMG48, arranged alphabetically mostly by name, or sometimes by award number. Deceased pensioners are also listed for the years 1877-1918.

After the disbandment of the force, those officers who were recommended for pensions are in lists by district, and in addition, separate lists were made for British and Irish officers. These are at HO 184/129-209. Not all records refer to the RIC directly, but are under the heading of Dublin Castle, and these are at CO 904/175-176. Particularly useful for digging into the earlier period, back in the Regency before the Irish Constabulary, are the superannuation lists given to Irish police: these are to be found in the House of Commons Sessional papers for 1831-1832, XXVI 465, and these provide name, period of service, the amount granted and the nature of the injury which led to the claim for superannuation.

As with all family history research, a fuller picture is needed, and all related social history is of immense value in understanding the nature of the work done by officers, and the administration process which controlled their working lives. Much of this material is available in the Dublin Castle records at CO 904 and the Irish office records at TNA, reference CO 906. This includes documentation of such aspects of police life as reports, civil disorder and force information such as circulars and instructions. This relates to major topics in Irish history, as the constabulary were known as the 'Irish gendarmerie' in some quarters, as they were involved in the Land Wars, the Fenian insurrections and later the 1916 rising and Civil War. At WO 35 there is material which provides excellent background information to these conflicts, and at HO 267 there are Home Office policy files with regard to Ireland. To back this up, and to read first-hand accounts of actions taken by the RIC, a search of the Times Digital Archive is recommended, particularly for the years c.1880-1900. The Ireland Files at T 192 cover the later years, 1920-1922 and there is also material in the Treasury archives, because the RIC worked with them also, on revenue, and they even did work as census enumerators. The Finance Files are at T 160 and the Pensions and Superannuation Files are at T 164, but as the research notes at TNA point out, there is no general index of names for these.

Any family history research for police in Ireland will inevitably present the reader with the challenge of understanding the complexity of modern Irish history, and although there is a massive library of books available in this area, there are other sources of great value, and in particular, the National Library of Ireland produces files of original sources, reprinted with guides, to many of more complicated areas of history. For instance, their file of *Historical Documents: The Past From the Press* consists of a collection of newspaper and journal cuttings, including topics in political life, leisure and sport. This series of folders has been in print since 1976, and there is a collection of facsimiles on the Land Wars, which is of especial value to researchers with police ancestors. These are available from The National Library of Ireland, Kildare Street, Dublin 2, Eire.

Upon Your Honour Sir!
The Duelling habit In Ireland 1750-1820

The notion of a face to face confrontation over a point of honour goes back a very long way. Where there has been a military elite or an aristocratic high culture, there have been fights concerning reputation. European life in the higher circles of power and status always had an element of preserving one's name and the honour attached. As Roderigo says to Iago in Othello, 'I have lost my reputation! I have lost the immortal part of myself and what remains is bestial..' The duel came into use in the forms we think of today, however, late in the sixteenth century; at that time there was a growing body of writing concerned with manners and courtly behaviour, notably the universally read *Il Libro del Cortegiano* (*The Courtier*) by Castiglioni.

There were codes of behaviour, governing the correct protocols for dealing with insults, and the mindset behind this stretches back to the time of trial by combat in the early medieval years. Duelling was banned under Cromwell, and also under Charles I and it was not until 1819 that the intricate and binding rules of duelling were taken from the statute books. The practice was universal, but certain places seemed to take to the custom with alacrity, and one of these locations was Ireland. Such was the esteem given to one who had taken part in a duel that in some quarters, such activity was thought to be essential to a proper education into the higher echelons of society. A question sometimes asked of a young man of quality was 'Did he blaze away?' The phrase was often used at the opening of the fight, one man shouting 'Blaze away!' to incite a response.

In 1777, the practice of duelling was so rife that Ireland had to sort out some kind of regulations. The men involved came up with an Irish Code and this was always referred to as the 'Twenty-six Commandments.' The interesting point about that event is that the men who decided on the commandments were at Clonmel assizes at the time. This happened at the summer assizes, and the rules were agreed on by men from five counties. The guidelines were so important that a copy of them, referred to as the 'commandments commandments' was ordered to be kept by a man, usually in his pistol case, so that if required, they could be consulted on points of proper behaviour and ritual. Maybe the men at Clonmel had done the legal business and had time to spare, so they put together some rules for what had always been a chaotic affair, with insults being given and responded to in all areas of the land where the gentry and their profligate sons were active.

The rules were very specific regarding the order of statements and events, so that, for instance, the first rule is complex and undoubtedly long-winded:

'The first offence requires the apology, although the retort may have been more offence than the insult. Example :A tells B he is impertinent; B retorts that he lies; yet A must make the first apology because he made the first offence and then (after one fire) B may explain away the retort by subsequent apology.'

The rules give us an insight into the wider culture of course, and to the various degrees of insults, such as number 10: *'Any insult to a lady under a gentleman's care and protection is to be considered as by one degree a greater offence than if given to the gentleman personally, and be regarded accordingly.'* Built into the code was the very practical direction that *'challenges must not be given at night'* thus avoiding, one assumes, the potential frequency of drunken challenges which would be regretted in the sobriety of the morning after.

In the last decades of the eighteenth century in Ireland, most duels were fought over insults, though political factors such as election encounters, were also common triggers to action; there were many deaths – one estimate suggests that the death rate was 1 in 4 at that time, although of course, there were very many confrontations which ended with no casualties.

The problem with the duel has always been that there was no scale of insults which was generally agreed on. As the historian V G Kiernan has explained: 'For some offences an exchange of two or more shots was held to be the minimum purgation. Cheating at cards was one of the crimes equivalent to a blow. An enlightened provision was that challenges should not be delivered bat night, *'for it is desirable to avoid all hot-headed proceedings.'* Irish heads were usually too well heated at night with claret.'

From the beginnings of recorded history in Ireland, there had been duels, even extending back to folklore and myth. But when the Restoration brought with it a conquest of the land by the Anglo-Irish class, duelling became a part of the ideology of their power and indeed their culture. A duel became a very common matter; the Victorian historian Froude referred to these people as *'Irish chiefs of the sixteenth century in modern costume.'* Being engaged in duelling was a crucially important part of the code of being a 'gentleman' of course and it was often said that a man was not able to take his place in the hierarchy of that power of the landed gentry until he had *'smelt powder.'*

In the eighteenth and early nineteenth centuries, there are numerous duels, some involved famous characters and some with very obscure people in the drama. Even Wolfe Tone acted as a second in a duel while at Trinity College, and one of his friends died in that encounter. So common was the habit that even the provost of the college was a duellist at one point. One particular area around the city was known for its duels – a place known as Clontarf Wood. The reputation of that place was that it was 'where men of heart go to bleed one another in duels.'

Irish Themes

One of the very last duels in Dublin took place in 1838, when a Galway man called O'Hara made a joke at the expense of Mr Robert Napoleon Finn. He refused to apologise and the duel had to go ahead, so seconds were appointed and the assignation was settled, to take place at North Bull, around three miles from Dublin. They arrived at the scene and put their coats on the sand; a man called Ireland was a witness and he later gave an account of what happened to William Le Fanu.

An experienced second said he would give the signal to fire and the two men stood at each side of him, ready to walk their twelve paces. What happened next was farcical. The second said that there would just be the one signal, the words, *'Ready, fire.'* But the nervous Finn, when he heard the man say the word fire, turned and pointed the pistol at him. The second told him to settle down, saying, *'Do you want to shoot me?'*

What followed was more like something from a melodrama:

'At the word "fire" Finn again lost his head, pulled the trigger of his pistol, which was pointed downwards, and lodged the bullet in the calf of his own leg. O'Hara, thinking that Finn had shot at him, immediately took aim at him, crying out, "For God's sake, don't fire. It was all a mistake!" But O'Hara did fire, and his bullet struck the ground close to Finn.'

Mr Ireland, watching from close by, was sprayed with sand, and then before any more developments could take place, four constables arrived and arrested everyone who was present. They were all put into carriages and taken back to Dublin. Ireland points out that Finn's injured leg was dangling out of a carriage to keep it cool. A Dublin joker said that Finn had gone to the Bull, got cow'd and shot the calf.

The famous Daniel O'Connell was also involved in a Dublin duel. After he criticised the Dublin corporation, he made enemies, and a character called D'Esterre challenged him to fight. O'Connell was a married man, having wed Mary, his cousin, in 1802. There was no doubt that D'Esterre had provoked the argument, but it went to the actual confrontation and he was shot. It took him a few days to die, but before he did so he exonerated O'Connell from any blame, and his second, Sir Edward Stanley, made it clear to O'Connell that there would be no prosecution. O'Connell was later to be on the wrong side of the law (while he was Mayor of Dublin) and was in jail for three months for conspiracy.

Aubrey de Vere, in his memoirs, says that 'In those days (1830s) a duel was the most mirthful of pastimes' and he described a meeting of two lawyers in Dublin who met at sunrise in Phoenix Park; 'one was the biggest and one the smallest' in Dublin society. But the big man had problems with his eyesight and said he could not see his opponent. The other instructed his second to draw a white chalk line of his own shape on the large 'carcass' of his opponent. Such jocularity in chatty memoirs does not even hint at the terrible tragedies that occurred in duels, such as the fight in 1786 between Robert Keon of Leitrim and George Nugent Reynolds. Keon and Reynolds arrived at the place for the duel before their seconds and went on without them; Keon shot Reynolds dead, then he was tried, found guilty and hanged, in March 1788.

In the late eighteenth century there had been some really prominent duels and some, such as a fight between Blaquerre and Bagenal in 1773 had such an effect that there was a public condemnation of the whole nasty business. But for a long time it was impossible to outlaw the practice; all that happened over the course of these years was that the fights were regulated, but not banned. There was always the added problem that when it was linked to army life and manners, there was a code of honour which ran contrary to the law.

Some duels were so high profile that they affected public opinion, and one notable confrontation between Flood and Agar led to duelling being given more general respect and support. This was because Flood, being accused of bribing magistrates, had such support and sympathy from the new middle classes that they took an interest in the case and in the words of one historian, the duel was 'the talk of the salons as well as the coffee houses.' The outcome was that duelling and its supporting code of honour, were understood and perhaps tolerated more by the public.

It has often been said and written that the notion of a duel, which is of course linked inextricably to notions of honour, reputation and class status, is deeply set in the Irish folklore and literature of earlier times. So much was this embedded in the later stereotypes of Irish character that the 'stage Irishman' of the eighteenth century English drama included the satirical depiction of the duelling temperament. The character of Sir Lucius O'Trigger in Sheridan's play *The Rivals* is typical of this. His name suggests his aggressive and volatile nature. That tradition of taking stock characters from Irish life and culture led to distortions and misunderstandings, but nevertheless, the historical record shows that Dublin people in these years had a penchant for settling disputes and matters of 'good name' by arranging a duel. The procedure and etiquette involved appealed so much to the general love of display and theatre that in terms of the media and the general civic gossip, at times a duel took its place as just another variety of slightly questionable but respected manly behaviour.

If we are to look for the kind of duel that would be more ordinary and typical, it would be the meeting between Standish O'Grady and Captain Smith in 1830. O'Grady, son of Edward O'Grady, chairman of the county of Waterford, was riding in Dawson Street when he smashed into a cabriolet driven by Captain Smith of the 32nd Regiment. O'Grady hit the officer's horse in order to free himself from the entanglement and Smith rounded on O'Grady and cracked him repeatedly with his own stick. O'Grady was merely a commissioner of bankrupts: Smith was a soldier, so the confrontation would be dangerous for the civilian generally, but he chased the cab and asked who had insulted him. Smith shouted out his name.

A message was sent by Lieutenant McNamara and they met at six in the morning, when O'Grady was shot, mortally wounded in the groin. Medical attention was given after he had been rushed to Richmond barracks, but he soon died.

The last death in a duel fought in Ireland is arguably that between Joseph Daunt of Kilcascan Castle, who was killed by his cousin from Manch House in 1826. This was, according to some, a duel fought over a suspected affair with the wife of the cousin. In England, as a contrast, the last duel on record happened in 1852 when a certain M. Barthelemey killed fellow Frenchman, M..Cournet at Egham in Surrey.

What does the story of duelling in Ireland in the Augustan and Regency years tell us? Mainly, such ritualistic affairs reflect the intricacy of the web of relationships in that social world of fast climbing and even more rapid falling from power or esteem. Reputations were a part of that fabric, but so were the demands made on people to maintain their status and name by established protocol in every walk of life. In an age of performance and display, of public showing-off of wealth and surface worth and vitality (as captured in the caricature art of Gillray and Rowlandson for instance), a duel was surely the extreme sensation, even more worthy of scandal and society chit-chat than an elopement or a suicide through disastrous gambling debts.

Further reading:
For one of the first detailed accounts, see W E H Lecky's *A History of Ireland in the Eighteenth Century* (Longman Green, 1892)
Barbara Holland,*Gentlemen's Blood* (Bloomsbury, 2003)
Richard Hopton,*Pistols at Dawn* (Portrait, 2007)
James Kelly,*That Damned Thing Called Honour* (Cork University press, 1995)
V G Kiernan,*The Duel in European History* (OUP,1989)

*

A Lawless Outrage:
Abductions in Eighteenth Century Ireland

My title refers to 'abductions' and in some ways this is a less frightening word than 'kidnapping' but in fact that terrible notion of forcible taking away, against the will, has run through European history, since the rape of the Sabine women in ancient Rome. The subject is an aspect of criminal history which has rarely been given any prominence. However, in recent years, it has caught the attention of popular writers and of academic historians.

If we survey patterns of crime in eighteenth century Britain, we find that, in an age with no professional effective police force, violent crime was rife and the value placed on human life was small indeed. We glamorize that Augustan age as a time of romantic highwaymen, dandies and rakes: a period of risk, adventure and dangerous streets. Partly, the reality was rather the same, but there was certainly no glamour in what lawyers would call 'crimes against the person' in that age of Swift, Johnson and Pope, when people were writing books about style, manners and proper behaviour. While the men of letters were chatting about Shakespeare in their spacious rooms, in the wilder areas of the kingdom there was barbarity- and that could be in the streets of London or the wilds of the mountains.

One crime from that era was notably rife in Ireland and Scotland, although it could happen anywhere: surely one of the most terrifying offences committed anywhere and at any time- abduction or kidnapping. Even today, the concepts of abduction and false imprisonment carry heavy penalties and attract the censure and disgust they deserve from law-abiding people. Back in the Georgian age, Ireland was one hot-spot of the crime, and the reasons are complicated. There also appears to be no pattern in these abductions, and explanations are hard to find.

In the time when the Old Bailey was the centre of attraction for everyone on both sides of the law, there were tradesmen about who were only too happy to cash in on the sensational and sad lives of villains – especially those whose lives had ended dangling on a rope at Tyburn. One such retailer was Richard Wam of the Bible and Sun at Warwick Lane, Amen Corner, London. Among his sick and bizarre items for sale there was a series of chapbooks with narratives on them, and one of these published in 1730 was this, as advertised:

'The case of Mr. Dan Kimberley, attorney at law, executed at Dublin, May 27, 1730, for assisting Bradock Mead to marry Bridget Rending, an heiress. Contained in his declaration and dying words, delivered to the Rev. Mr. Derry, at the place of execution, and recommended to Dean Percival, John Hacket, Esq', and two other gentlemen, to see it published. Price: three pence.'

Behind that smart piece of advertising there lies not only the complex tale of a learned and educated man who fell into deep trouble, but also a story typical of its age and place – one more abduction in hundreds, a trade (and a crime) totally heartless and unscrupulous – and of course, a capital offence. Kimberley's last dying speech tract was headed, 'Daniel Kimberly, Gentleman' Those words were unusual for a gallows tale, and his date with death was as meticulously recorded as the events of his own story: *'Executed at St Stephen's Green on Wednesday, May 27th, 1730 at 38 minutes past three o'clock in the afternoon.'*

The famous historian of eighteenth century Ireland, W E H Lecky, in his account of the spate of abductions of heiresses in that time, explains how many people ascribed them to sectarian enmity, yet he finds little evidence of that. But there were certainly many varieties of abduction, and whatever their nature, they were brutal and cruel. At its worst, an abduction could be like this one, as described by Lecky:

'On a Sunday in the June of 1756, the Rev. John Armstrong was celebrating divine service in the Protestant church in the town of Tipperary, Susannah Grove being among the congregation. In the midst of the service Henry Grady, accompanied by a body of men armed with blunderbuses, pistols, and other weapons, called out to the congregation that anyone who stirred would be shot, struck the clergyman on the arm with a hanger and . . . hastening to the pew where Susannah was sitting, dragged her out . . .'

But we are not dealing with this variety in Kimberly's story, and, as Lecky points out, the Kimberly case is unusual because he was a Protestant, pointing out that '

Among the few persons who were executed for abduction in Ireland was an attorney named Kimberly, at a time when no-one but a professing Protestant could be enrolled in that profession.'

Here then, we have a case of a lawyer and a Protestant being hanged for an offence for which few were hanged. What was so heinous about this particular abduction? Or did Kimberly have powerful enemies?

His own account of the events of the abduction of Bridget Reading (not *Rending*, as the London printer had it) is expectedly, full of bad luck stories and of his being an innocent dupe. Making sense of Kimberly's own garbled and complicated account of what happened, there emerges a bare outline of a plausible story: he was a lawyer and so would have appeared to be hardly a 'heavy' when it came to applying some pressure on the intended abduction and forced marriage of your Bridget Reading, for that is what lies at the heart of this story. Kimberly was contacted by an unscrupulous adventurer called Braddock Mead, with an assignment of visiting the nurse who had the guardianship of Bridget. Now, Kimberly argued that the old couple who had Bridget in care were also after her inheritance, and he said that he was told 'there was a considerable sum of money due to her... she never having received a penny from her father, who was an ill man.'

The lawyer then found out that Mead, back in London, had more knowledge of Bridget's situation than he had at first said because he took out articles with a man called Dodamy with a plan to sell Bridget's estate for the then huge sum of £3,600. The pressure was then on Kimberly to get a desired result in his negotiations to prise Bridget from her guardian and to speed her to the altar with Mead. Again and again, Kimberly insisted that there had been no forced marriage: 'soon after, and by my consent, and inducement, Mead applied to said Bridget by way of courtship and on 11th April, 1728, said Mead married her in Dublin, when and where no force, threats, or compulsion was made use of by any person towards said Bridget to come into said marriage.'

Understanding this case is all a matter of believing Kimberly was 'sold out' to the law or not. His argument was that Mead was largely responsible for duping him and setting him up, as he was seen as the actual agent of the affair, and so would be assumed to have used force on the girl. When Mead was arrested and imprisoned and the network was about to be destroyed (and heads to roll) Mead was threatened by Mr Reading to apply a charge of rape against him unless he had the marriage annulled, Kimberly was apparently 'stooged.' He did understand that the right moves had been attempted, though. Applications were made to the Doctor's Commons, and though the intentions may have been good, to dissolve the contract, perhaps the Doctors' Commons was not the right place to go. Later, Dickens was to call that institution of Doctors of Law 'a cosy, dozy, old-fashioned and time-forgotten, sleepy-headed little family party.'

As with all such convoluted narratives of crime, it all depends who is believed at the time, and by the people who matter. Daniel Kimberly was clearly not believed; we have his side of the story, but we also have the weight of history and statistics to show how hard the authorities were coming down on abductions of heiresses. It may be that, in the end, Kimberly was being harshly punished as a precedent to other professional gentleman not to be involved in that nefarious and amoral trade.

He faced his death on the scaffold with courage, offering to give dramatic entertainment to the crowd. He even ended his speech with the surprising attitude of forgiveness: 'As for my prosecutors, or such as have persecuted me. Or fought any perjurious or indirect ways to take away my life, I freely forgive them.' Reading between the lines, there is still rancour there, and a 'spin' towards showing himself in a better light than his enemies. But, as with many others in his final minutes, his main concern was for his reputation: 'In order to prevent the publishing of any false or spurious accounts of me... I do therefore humbly entreat my very worthy friends, the rev. Dean Percival, Mr Derry, John Hacket, Edmund Fenner... to order the printing and publishing of this declaration.'

He did have some friends (Dean Percival has gone down in history as one of the men who lampooned Jonathan Swift in a satirical poem) but clearly their exertions were not strenuous enough to save him from the gallows.

As to trends in abductions generally, Lecky did his own investigation back in 1890 and his conclusion was, after dealing with the theory that most were sectarian, and that Catholic abductions were condoned by priests, he concluded that 'The truth is that the crime was merely the natural product of a state of great lawlessness and barbarism, and it continued in some parts of Ireland later than in other countries, because, owing to circumstances described in the present chapter [the lack of authority impinging on the state of affairs] the formation of habits of order and respect for law was unnaturally retarded.'

Lecky looked into archives at Dublin Castle, and there he found that in the presentments of grand juries for the years 1700-1760, 28 cases were of abduction, and in only four of these is there any evidence that a Protestant victim was taken away by a Catholic band of abductors. He notes that these presentments were created by

Protestants of course, and the depositions therein would be sworn by Protestant families, so as he says, 'We may be sure that no element of sectarian aggravation that could plausibly be alleged is omitted.' He weighs the evidence of the material carefully and sees no certainty that the old tales of Catholic dominated abductions had truth in them.

Although there were undoubtedly many abductions related to profits from marriage at the time, as in Kimberly's case, a factor that must be recalled was that an Act of 1745 made marriages celeb rated by priests between Protestants and Catholics null and void.'

But the stories and myths went on, into the regency years. Arthur Young, the agrarian traveller and farmer, in his tour of Britain at the turn of the eighteenth century, noted that abductions were fairly common, but again, he has no explanation which relates to sectarian violence. What is of interest with regard to how the tales graduated to perhaps fictional proportions is that the English Victorian historian, J A Froude, wrote of them in his popular work, *The English in Ireland in the Eighteenth Century.* Froude wanted the historiography to be one of religious interplay and depredation. Lecky took the opposite view. But in the end, as Kimberly's case shows, the reasons for the crime being fairly common across the centuries is a very different one.

We owe this largely to research done by James Kelly in his work, 'The Abduction of Women of Fortune in Eighteenth Century Ireland' in which he explains the economic basis of this nefarious crime. Kelly notes that going back to an Act of 1634 which stated that those who 'take away... and deflower.. maidens that be inheritors' were subject to imprisonment for between two and five years and also, their next of kin would be disinherited. In other words, the economic factor is uppermost. Partly for this reason, there were such things as arranged abductions, involving no rape, for instance. Kelly explains that a writer of 1682 telling tales of abduction often uses what were in fact 'ritualistic' ones – not forcible abduction. This means that, although a girl had rebuffed a suitor, the father and family had actually pressurised her into relenting, and agreed that an apparent abduction should take place. This seems not dissimilar to a situation akin to Shakespeare's *The Taming of the Shrew* in that a girl was designed to be off-loaded to a suitor, even though he might be rough type, likely to step over moral or legal lines, to get his woman.

An account from the later fifteenth century explains what this was: 'When a man is in love with a woman but is repulsed... he often has recourse to the following stratagem. He causes a report to be spread in the neighbourhood that he intends to carry her off. This seldom fails of gaining the point. He is now permitted to pay his addresses without interruption, and is generally looked on by the family as a true and sincere love...'

The debate on Irish abductions brings out several interesting elements of the social and legal history, not the least of these being that historians of the past have wanted to find sectarian aspects of the events – common of course in all areas of Irish writing – but this also highlights the now (with hindsight) obvious and rather clumsy bias of Victorian writers on this very emotional theme. This partly falls in line with the disgusting representations of Irish people as in Victorian periodicals and the literary stereotypes, but we also have here an example of how some of the most heinous crimes of the past were sometimes interpreted without any real feeling for the human situation beneath the legal situation. That is, perhaps, left to the novelists and documentary writers. Yet the case of abductions presents the reader of Irish history with something open to a number of interpretations, while it must be said that in the end, much of the answer lies in the parental machinations in a period of paternal governance, when the family unit was part of a clan, for self-preservation and survival.

In the novels of Jane Austen, the reader may be asked to be appalled at the event of two young lovers engaging in a dangerous elopement, following romantic attachment rather than economic and social sense, and yet the supposed opposite situation of a forced kidnapping for a beneficial marriage was arguably too much for popular fiction. Though it may at times have had a willing, artificial aspect, on the whole it was a 'barbarous' practice as Lecky expressed it, and historians are now engaged in digging for further truths about the practice.

Further Reading

J A Froude, *The English in Ireland in the Eighteenth Century* (Longmans Green, 1886)

James Kelly, *The Abduction of Women in Eighteenth Century Ireland Eighteenth Century Ireland* (Eighteenth Century Ireland Society, 1994)

W E H Lecky, *A History of Ireland in the Eighteenth Century* (Longmans Green, 1892)

General Bibliography

BOOKS

I have organised this according to categories of books and sources, using and sometimes describing how these relate to criminal history. Most are in print but some extremely useful works in this area are out of print; often that is the case, I have selected only those volumes which are, without question, especially useful in the search for criminal ancestors.

A Note on Primary Printed Sources

Throughout the book, there have been references to classic works of crime narrative, and also to some hard-to-find texts such as autobiographies and biographies of criminals. Much of this is accessible online through the Old Bailey sessions records, but these may be worthwhile also:

The Newgate Calendar (Various editions) Typical of these is the Folio edition, with old engravings, edited by Sir Norman Birkett in 1951.

Philip Priestley's *Victorian Prison Lives* (Pimlico, 1999) uses a large number of memoirs in order to reconstruct the daily lives of people in gaol in that period. Other useful biographical material on the lives of judges, lawyers, prisoners and criminals are:

Bamford, Samuel *Passages in the Life of a Radical* (Oxford, 1984)

Douglas, Robert *At Her Majesty's Pleasure* (Hodder, 2007)

Humphreys, Sir Travers *A Book of Trials* (Pan, 1953)

Humphreys, Sir Travers *Criminal Days* (Hodder and Stoughton, 1945)

Reference- General Crime History and Family History

Looking into crimes from the past, and tracing ancestors involved in any prominent way, can involve delving into any number of secondary, 'off –shoot' sources. Sometimes, I have enlarged the scope of enquiry on a particular case and found, by sheer serendipity, material in such places as memoirs or letters which have enriched the eventual narrative I assembled.

Sources range from the 'direct route' through court records, down to the personal accounts from witnesses. Persistence is required, and also an openness to searching across laterally, from the trial records for instance. The effort is worth it, as there is almost always the joy of finding an unexpected depth to a story, or even the discovery of your family or local tale as something that linked to a major national event.

Much may now be achieved from your office at home, as more and more records are put online. Yet still there is a limitation in this: the full story may need as much closeness to the place and people as possible, and if travel is possible and not too expensive, then actually seeing and noting the location of a crime is invaluable.

There is also the question of the value of out of print books. Naturally, this kind of addition to research may be expensive, but I have to admit that, over the years of research into this area of social history, I have had the most significant revelations about people from the past in the dusty volumes of biography, journals and letters found in long-forgotten places where second-hand books go to linger until someone hunts them out.

The Annual Register- from the early eighteenth century, still in existence, but for full crime reports and trials reports, the numbers up to the mid nineteenth centuries are the most useful.

Cyriax, Oliver *The Penguin Encyclopaedia of Crime* (Penguin, 1993

Hawkings, David T *Criminal Ancestors* A Guide to historical criminal records In England and Wales (History Press, 2010))

Paley, Ruth and Fowler, Simon *Family Skeletons* The National Archives2005

Pearsall, Mark *The National Archives Family History Companion* (TNA 2007

Family History

Bell, Gail *The Poison Principle – a memoir of family secrets and literary Poisoning* (Pan Books, 2002)

Blatchford, Robert & Elizabeth (Ed.) *The Family and Local History Handbook* Robert Blatchford Publishing (This is now at volume number 14 and provides an excellent compendium of articles on all aspects of the subject. As well as an archive reference section, featuring police records and others, there are always features on criminal history in each volume.)

Busby, Sian *The Cruel Mother* (Short Books, 2004) (This is a family memoir combined with a research project based on Sian's Great-grandmother who was sentenced to an indefinite term in Broadmoor in 1919)

Chater, Kathy *How to Trace Your Family Tree* (Hermes House, 2003)

Fowler, Simon (Ed.) *Starting Out in Family History* (TNA 2008)

Iredale, David and Barrett, John *Discovering Your Family Tree* (Shire, 2002)

(This is particularly useful on justices of the peace and on the courts)

Landale, James *Duel – a true story of death and honour* (Canongate, 2005)

(In 1826 a businessman, David Landale, shot his bank manager dead in a duel. The author delves into Scottish family history to follow the trail; David Landale was found not guilty)

Local History

Carter, Paul and Thompson, Kate *Sources for Local Historians* (Phillimore, 2005)

(This is excellent on information regarding assize courts and police. It is also arguably the best book for the reproduction of documents of all kinds)

Friar, Stephen *The Sutton Companion to Local History* (Sutton, 2001)

Richardson, John *The Local Historian's Encyclopaedia* (Historical Publications, 1974)

(Although this is out of print, it is worth tracing because it has sections arranged alphabetically, including a Law and Order section and other related sections such as welfare, militia etc.)

Social History/History of Crime and Law

Arieno, Marlene *Victorian Lunatics: a social epidemiology of mental illness in mid-nineteenth century England* (Susquehanna University Press, 1989)

Barnard, Sylvia M *Viewing the Breathless Corpse. Coroners and inquests in Victorian Leeds* (Words@Woodmere, 2001)

Birkenhead, Earl of, *Famous Trials* (Hutchinson, 1925)

(This has accounts of several high-profile trials, covering treason, murder, fraud and sedition.

Cobley, John *The Crimes of the First Fleet Convicts* (Sydney, 1970)

Cook, Chris, *Britain in the Nineteenth Century 1815-1914* (Routledge, 2005)

Cowie, L W *The Wordsworth Dictionary of Social History* (Wordsworth, 1996)

Denning, Lord *Landmarks in the Law* (Butterworths, 1984)

Emsley, Clive *Crime and Society in England 1750-1900* (Longman, 1987)

Gregory, Jeremy and Stevenson, John *Britain in the Eighteenth Century* (Routledge, 2007)

Hibbert, Christopher *The Roots of EvilA social history of crime and punishment* (Sutton, 2003)

Hughes, Robert *The Fatal Shore* (Collins Harvill, 1987)

Jackson, Lee *A Dictionary of Victorian London* (Anthem, 2006)

McKie, David *Jabez. The Rise and Fall of a Victorian Rogue* (Atlantic Books, 2004)

Morgan, Gwenda and Rushton, Peter *Eighteenth Century Criminal Transportation* (Palgrave, 2004)

Morris, Norval and Rothman, David J *The Oxford History of the Prison* (Oxford, 1998)

Naphy, William *Sex Crimes from Renaissance to Enlightenment* (Tempus, 2002)

Nicholl, Charles *The Lodger* (Penguin, 2007)

Osborne, Bertram *Justices of the Peace 1361-1848* (Oxford, 1977)

Porter, Bernard *Plots and Paranoia – a history of political espionage in Britain 1790 – 1988* (Routledge, 1989)

(This is excellent for the crime of sedition in the Regency period and for treason in later times).
Rees, Sian *The Floating Brothel* (Headline, 2001)
Saul, Nigel *A Companion to Medieval England1066-1485* (Tempus, 2005)
Sharpe, J A *Crime in Early Modern England 1550-1750* (Longman, 1984)
Summers, Ann *Damned Whores and God's Police* (Melbourne, 1982)

Newspapers, Journals and Periodicals
General
For newspaper reports of crimes and trials, *The Times Digital Archives* and *The Guardian* Archives are well worth the effort and expense of subscription. In addition there is the online facility of the *British Library's Nineteenth Century British Newspapers/Periodicals* search process.

These periodicals are worth looking at for features on all aspects of crime and law in their period:
Daily Graphic (this has police court features and reports from other courts)
Gentleman's Magazine Household Narrative (for the 1850s and 1860s)
Illustrated London News
Strand Magazine (1890s in particular)

Specific articles on crimes and criminal law
Academic journals often have excellent features on the social context of crime, at all stages in history, so the indexes of social

history journals are always worth searching, and the case is the same for journals of criminology or the Prison Service.

Ancestors magazine issue 17 Dec. 2003 Special issue of crime and punishment. (This issue has features on quarter sessions, justices of the peace and a transportation case study

Heather, Chris 'Licences at Large' in *Ancestors* issue 74 Oct. 2008 (This is a special feature on the newly accessible database at TNA on female prisoners.)

Keneally, Thomas *Convict Nation BBC History magazine* July, 2006 pp. 35-40

Kesselring, Krista *Detecting Death Disguised History Today* April, 2006 pp. 20-26 (This explains issues related to early coroners' courts)

King, Peter *The Summary Courts and Social relations in Eighteenth Century England Past and Present* May 2004 Number 183pp. 125-172 (This is a very comprehensive survey of the smaller courts and how they worked)

Thomas, Jenny *Tracing Your Criminal Ancestors* in *Who Do You Think you Are* magazine BBC Issue 3 Dec. 2007

Websites

These listings are sites with material on criminal records and on related social historical subjects which prove valuable in research in this area.

The major general sites are mostly not included.
Access to Archives www.a2a.org.uk
Archives Hub www.archiveshub.ac.uk

Archives Network Wales www.archivesnetworkwales.info
Australian Family History Compendium www.cohsoft.com.au/afhc
Australian national Archives www.naa.gov.au
BBC Family History www.bbc.co.uk/history/familyhistory
Blacksheep Ancestors www.Blacksheepancestors.com
The Borthwick Institute www.york.ac.uk/inst/bihr
British History Online www.british-history.ac.uk
British Library www.bl.uk/familyhistory.html
Cemeteries of Australia www.ozgenonline.com/aust_ cemeteries
Chartist Ancestors www.Chartists.net
Clergy of the Church of England Database www.theclergydatabase.org.uk
Convict records in Australia www. Coraweb.com.au/convict.html
Federation of Family History Societies www.ffhs.org.uk
The Genealogist www.thegenealogist.co.uk
Guardian and Observer Digital Archive archive-guardian.co.uk
Irish Abroad www.irishabroad.com/yourroots
Irish Newspaper Archives www.irishnewsarchive.com
Lambeth Palace Library www.lambethpalacelibrary.org
London Generations www.cityoflondon.gov.uk/londonGenerations
Medieval English Genealogy www.medievalgenealogy.org.uk
Metropolitan Police History www.met.police.uk/history
The National Archives www.nationalarchives.go.uk
National Archives of Scotland www.nas.gov.uk
National Library of Wales www.llgc.org.uk
Old Bailey Trials www.oldbaileyonline.org
Scotland's people www.scotland'speople.gov.uk
Trade Union Ancestors www.unionancestors.co.uk

Victorian Web www. Victorianweb.org.
A Web of English History www.historyhome.co.uk
Workhouses www.workhouses.org.

**